200 vegan

hamlyn | all colour cookbook

200 vegan recipes

Emma Frost & Nichola Palmer

An Hachette UK Company
www.hachette.co.uk

First published in Great Britain in 2014 by Hamlyn
a division of Octopus Publishing Group Ltd
Endeavour House, 189 Shaftesbury Avenue
London WC2H 8JY
www.octopusbooks.co.uk

ISBN: 978-0-60062-980-1

A CIP catalogue record for this book is available from the
British Library

Printed and bound in China

10 9 8 7 6 5 4 3 2 1

Both metric and imperial measurements have
been given in all recipes. Use one set of measurements
only, and not a mixture of both.

Standard level spoon measurements are used in all recipes
1 tablespoon = 15 ml spoon
1 teaspoon = 5 ml spoon

Ovens should be preheated to the specified temperature –
if using a fan-assisted oven, follow the manufacturer's
instructions for adjusting the time and temperature.

Fresh herbs should be used unless otherwise stated.
Freshly ground black pepper should be used unless
otherwise stated.

This book includes dishes made with nuts and nut
derivatives. It is advisable for people with known allergic
reactions to nuts and nut derivatives or those who may be
potentially vulnerable to these allergies, such as pregnant
and nursing mothers, invalids, the elderly, babies and
children, to avoid dishes made with these. It is prudent to
check the labels of all pre-prepared ingredients for the
possible inclusion of nut derivatives.

contents

introduction

introduction

Eating a diet that is totally plant based, without animal foods or by-products, has never been easier and is no longer the quirky preference only of those living an alternative lifestyle. Most major supermarkets and high street health-food shops sell a good selection of dairy-free milks, creams and spreads as well as seeds and whole grains, so all the ingredients you need can be incorporated into your normal shopping routine.

If you are contemplating becoming vegan, have been vegan for years or will be cooking for a vegan friend or member of the family, whatever your situation we hope you find inspiration in these easy recipes for every occasion. Being free from animal products, these recipes are also suitable for those with a dairy and/or egg intolerance or allergy.

Eating a healthy vegan diet

More and more of us are turning to a vegan diet, whether on the grounds of personal health or animal welfare, and it can be something you can introduce and adopt gradually. You may wish to start with one week a month and then increase your vegan eating pattern over a period of time to reach a level that you are comfortable with, or you may be happy to become completely vegan from the start. You may also find it a good weight-loss diet – a diet rich in whole grains and fibre from fruit and vegetables will keep you feeling fuller for longer with less temptation to snack between meals.

The key to a healthy vegan diet is to eat a variety of foods, including fruit, vegetables, leafy greens, whole grains, nuts, seeds and pulses, to make every plateful of food a colourful one, which will indicate you are well on the way to achieving a good balance of nutrients.

A vegan diet is not without treats though – just turn to the Breads and Baking section (see page 172) and also the Desserts section (see page 202) for a range of delicious cakes, muffins, breads, biscuits and puddings.

The main nutrients for a healthy vegan diet are found in the following foods:

Protein

Soya is the best source of protein, containing all the essential amino acids needed by the body. Tofu, made from fermented soya beans, is a good meat substitute and can be cooked in stews and stir-fries, grilled and marinated, as well as crumbled to make a decent replacement for scrambled eggs. Other good sources of protein are peas, edamame (soya) beans, peanuts, chickpeas, grains such as quinoa (pronounced keenwa) and wheat, nuts and seeds.

Vitamin B12

Found in yeast extract (Marmite) and often added to breakfast cereals and plant milks.

Calcium

Added to plant milks and found in green vegetables, whole grains and bread.

Vitamin D

Needed for the absorption of calcium, your body makes its own vitamin D from sunlight, so it is important to get outdoors for a walk every day if possible, but vitamin D is also added to dairy-free spreads.

Iron

Good sources are lentils, tofu, kidney beans, chickpeas, quinoa and dried fruits such as dried apricots and figs and prunes.

Omega-3 fatty acids

Usually found in oily fish, but plant sources are leafy green vegetables, nuts and oils such as flaxseed (linseed), olive, avocado, groundnut and rapeseed.

Frozen vegetables are a great time saver, prepared and chopped ready to use, and because they are frozen within hours of picking, they often contain more vitamins than fresh, especially if the latter are a few days old.

Fresh herbs give instant colour to cooked grains, add freshness to salads and flavour to salad dressing and sauces. Grow your own if you can, as they are so much cheaper and are there to hand whenever you need them. They don't take up much space – even a windowsill will do. Just keep them well watered and they will last a long time. If you do buy them in packs, any leftovers can be chopped and frozen in ice cube trays topped up with water or oil. Just pop them out straight into the pan as you need them.

Making life easier

Keeping a well-stocked store cupboard with a variety of canned beans and tomatoes, whole grains, seeds, nuts and oils, and a freezer of vegetables and fruits will help you to maintain healthy eating habits with little effort.

The cost of nuts, seeds and oils can all add up, so make sure you keep track of the best-before dates, as the oils in all these products will deteriorate and turn rancid after a while. If you buy in bulk, nuts and seeds can be frozen to keep them fresh. Toasting nuts and seeds in a dry frying pan will refresh them and bring out their flavour.

Canned beans and tomatoes have a long shelf life and have as much nutritional value as dried (beans) and fresh (tomatoes), so keep a good supply for rustling up a quick chilli, soup or pasta sauce.

Vegan alternatives

There are lots of options to choose from when looking for non-animal-based alternatives to cooking and serving staples, so take the opportunity to explore and experiment to find which you like best for different uses.

Milk

There is a wealth of different dairy-free milks available in both chilled and long-life forms including soya, almond, hazelnut, coconut, rice and oat. The choice mainly comes down to personal taste and flavour preference as well as any intolerances or allergies, such as nut, you may have.

Some plant milks come in sweetened and unsweetened versions, so check the label before you buy – if it doesn't state unsweetened on the pack, it is usually sweetened. Coconut milk with its mild coconutty flavour is ideal for making rice pudding and for creamy-style curries. Rice milk is one of the thinner milks with a light flavour, good for pouring over cereals and making coffee, but one of the least stable when heated.

Nut, soya and oat milks are good for baking and cooking, as they add a creamy richness to muffins, cakes and sauces.

Cream

Non-dairy cream is usually made from soya, oats, coconut or nuts, and just as in the dairy versions they are richer than the milks. Good for pouring over desserts and for making creamy savoury and sweet sauces for pasta, pies, custard and ice cream.

Cheese

Made from blends of potato starch, vegetable oil and soya protein, dairy-free cheeses are available in mozzarella, Cheddar, Parmesan and Edam styles. Ready-grated dairy-free mozzarella is handy for sprinkling over pizzas,

pasta bakes and jacket potatoes. Dairy-free cheeses are not so readily available in supermarkets, so a visit to a health-food shop or online website is required to source them.

Cooking fats and oils
Whey and buttermilk are often used in spreads made from olive oil and sunflower oil, so check that they are completely dairy-free before buying. Virgin coconut oil, which is solid

at room temperature, is a healthy oil to use for baking and frying, as is rapeseed oil and sunflower oil. Extra virgin olive oil and avocado oil are delicious for drizzling over roasted vegetables and for making salad dressings.

Yogurt
Soya yogurt is the most widely available dairy-free yogurt in a choice of natural and vanilla- and fruit-flavoured versions. Natural is great for topping breakfast granola or for making savoury dips such as tzatziki with garlic, mint and cucumber to serve as a snack with raw vegetable sticks and wholemeal pitta breads or with spicy foods as a cooling relish.

Honey
As honey is a by-product from bees, it isn't suitable for a vegan diet. A good alternative is agave nectar, a plant-based syrup, which is also sweeter than honey, so you can use less. Drizzle it straight from the squeezy jar over porridge or pancakes, or use in cooking. Maple syrup is another delicious alternative to honey with a slight caramel flavour, making it perfect for desserts and biscuits.

Eggs
You may think that cooking without eggs rules out cakes, muffins, pancakes, mayonnaise and custard in your life, but amazingly it doesn't. It is possible to buy egg substitute from health-food shops, but for the recipes in this book eggs have been replaced with cider vinegar or

for a vegan diet. Grains such as quinoa, bulgar wheat, barley and spelt add a nutty flavour and plenty of texture to dishes such as risottos and salads and stuffings for vegetables. They are also an easy way to thicken soups and stews for a more substantial meal.

Protein-packed lentils make rich, warming casseroles and soups as well as salads and side dishes. Brown and green lentils tend to retain their shape when cooked and so are good for salads and stuffings, whereas red split lentils cook to a softer purée and therefore make an ideal thickener for soups and stews, and are used for making dhal.

Seeds
They may be tiny but seeds are packed with protein, fibre, iron, vitamins and omega-3 fatty acids, which means that they are well worth

lemon juice in cakes and muffins and baking powder in pancakes. You will be surprised how delicious they are and easy to make. For a creamy mayonnaise-style salad dressing, you can use silken tofu blended with lemon juice or a little vinegar.

Wholesome vegan options
Given that grains, pulses and seeds are a vital source of protein in a vegan diet, it makes sense to make the best of their considerable potential.

Whole grains and lentils
Whole grains contain more iron and B vitamins, and are richer in fibre and protein than refined ones, so are a preferable choice

generously sprinkling over salads, pilau rice, risottos and breakfast cereals and mixing into bread dough and muffin mixes. Chia, sesame, pumpkin, sunflower, hemp and golden flaxseed (linseed) are all great nutrition and flavour boosters.

Checking food labels

When shopping, look for the Vegan Society logo or products that state that they are suitable for vegans on the packaging. If you are unsure whether an item is vegan, check the ingredients list for any of the following, in which case the product will be unsuitable: Gelatine (made from animal bones), honey, whey (liquid left after milk has been curdled), cochineal (a pink colouring made from crushed insects), Quorn (suitable for vegetarians but not vegans, as it contains egg), Worcestershire sauce (contains anchovies), Thai fish sauce (made from fermented fish and shellfish), Thai curry paste (usually contains fish sauce), Bovril (made from beef), ghee in curries and naan breads (clarified butter)

'Hidden' non-vegan ingredients

The following products need a careful ingredients check, as they might catch you out:

Pasta, especially fresh pasta – check that it is egg free

Noodles – avoid egg noodles and choose rice noodles instead

Plain dark chocolate – may contain some milk

Beers, wines and cider – some are filtered using animal products

Vegetarian burgers and sausages – may contain eggs, milk or Quorn

Sweets and marshmallows – often made with gelatine

Cereal bars and breakfast cereals – may be sweetened with honey

breakfast & brunches

mango & orange smoothie

Serves **2**
Preparation time **10 minutes**

1 ripe **mango**, peeled, stoned
   and chopped, or 150 g
   (5 oz) frozen **mango chunks**
150 g (5 oz) **natural soya
   yogurt**
150 ml (¼ pint) **orange juice**
finely grated rind and juice of
   1 **lime**
2 teaspoons **agave nectar**, or
   to taste

Blend together the mango, yogurt, orange juice, lime rind and juice and agave nectar in a blender or food processor until smooth.

Pour into 2 glasses and serve.

For ginger banana smoothie, blend together 1 ripe banana, 1.5 cm (¾ inch) piece of fresh root ginger, peeled and grated, 150 g (5 oz) natural soya yogurt and 150 ml (¼ pint) orange or mango juice in a blender or food processor until smooth. Sweeten to taste with agave nectar, pour into 2 glasses and serve.

toasted muesli with coconut chips

Serves **8**
Preparation time **15 minutes**
Cooking time **15–20 minutes**

350 g (11½ oz) **rolled oats**
75 g (3 oz) **coconut chips**
75 g (3 oz) **sunflower seeds**
200 g (7 oz) **pumpkin seeds**
150 g (5 oz) **flaked almonds**
100 g (3½ oz) **hazelnuts**
4 tablespoons **maple syrup**
2 tablespoons **sunflower oil**
250 g (8 oz) **sultanas**
75 g (3 oz) **dried figs**, roughly
  chopped

To serve
soya milk
raspberries

Mix together the oats, coconut chips, sunflower and pumpkin seeds, flaked almonds and hazelnuts in a large bowl.

Transfer half the muesli mixture to a separate bowl. Mix the maple syrup and oil together in a jug, then pour over the remaining half of the muesli and toss really well to lightly coat all the ingredients.

Line a large roasting tin with baking parchment, scatter over the syrup-coated muesli and spread out in a single layer. Bake in a preheated oven, 150°C (300°F), Gas Mark 2, for 15–20 minutes, stirring occasionally, until golden and crisp.

Leave to cool completely, then toss with the uncooked muesli and the dried fruit. Store in airtight storage jars. Serve with soya milk and raspberries.

For soft cinnamon muesli with almonds & banana, mix together 350 g (11½ oz) rolled oats, 250 g (8 oz) sultanas, 200 g (7 oz) each pumpkin seeds and toasted blanched almonds, 100 g (3½ oz) soft dried banana slices, 75 g (3 oz) each pitted dried dates and sunflower seeds and 2 teaspoons ground cinnamon in a large bowl. Store in airtight storage jars. Serve with soya milk or soya yogurt and fresh fruit if liked.

mushroom tofu scramble

Serves **4**

Preparation time **15 minutes**

Cooking time **5 minutes**

2 tablespoons **rapeseed** or
olive oil

200 g (7 oz) **chestnut
mushrooms**, trimmed and
quartered

250 g (8 oz) **firm tofu**,
drained, patted dry and
crumbled

125 g (4 oz) **baby plum
tomatoes**, halved

1 tablespoon **mushroom
ketchup**

3 tablespoons chopped **flat
leaf parsley**

salt and **pepper**

hash browns, to serve

Heat the oil in a frying pan, add the mushrooms and
cook over a high heat, stirring frequently, for 2 minutes
until browned and softened. Add the tofu and cook,
stirring, for 1 minute.

Add the tomatoes to the pan and cook for 2 minutes
until starting to soften. Stir in the mushroom ketchup
and half the parsley and season with salt and pepper.

Serve immediately with hash browns, sprinkled with
the remaining parsley.

For spinach & sweetcorn tofu scramble, heat
2 tablespoons rapeseed or olive oil in a frying pan.
Add 250 g (8 oz) firm tofu, drained, patted dry and
crumbled, with 1 teaspoon smoked paprika and cook,
stirring, for 2 minutes until hot. Add 75 g (3 oz) frozen
or drained canned sweetcorn kernels and heat through
for 1 minute, then add 250 g (8 oz) spinach and heat
until just wilted. Season with salt and pepper and serve
with hash browns or toasted sourdough bread.

carrot & apple muffins

Makes **12**
Preparation time **20 minutes**
Cooking time **15–20 minutes**

300 g (10 oz) **self-raising
  flour**
1½ teaspoons **bicarbonate
  of soda**
½ teaspoon **salt**
1½ teaspoons **ground
  cinnamon**
1 teaspoon **ground ginger**
75 g (3 oz) **raisins**
150 g (5 oz) **light muscovado
  sugar**
1 tablespoon **poppy seeds**
275 ml (9 fl oz) **almond milk**
100 ml (3½ fl oz) **olive oil,**
  plus extra for oiling (optional)
1 tablespoon **cider vinegar**
1 **dessert apple**, cored and
  coarsely grated
1 **carrot**, peeled and coarsely
  grated

Line 12 holes of a muffin tin with paper cases or lightly oil and line the bases with discs of baking parchment.

Sift the flour, bicarbonate of soda, salt, cinnamon and ginger together into a bowl. Stir in the raisins, sugar and poppy seeds.

Mix the almond milk, oil and vinegar together in a jug. Add to the dry ingredients and lightly stir together until just mixed. Quickly fold in the apple and carrot, then divide the mixture between the paper cases or the holes of the muffin tin.

Bake straight away in a preheated oven, 190°C (375°F), Gas mark 5, for 15–20 minutes until well risen and golden. Transfer to a wire rack to cool. Store the muffins for up to for 2–3 days in an airtight container, or freeze.

For carrot, pine nut & orange muffins, prepare a muffin tin as above. Sift 300 g (10 oz) self-raising flour, 1½ teaspoons bicarbonate of soda and ½ teaspoon salt together into a bowl. Stir in 50 g (2 oz) toasted pine nuts, 150 g (5 oz) light muscovado sugar and the finely grated rind of 1 orange. Mix 275 ml (9 fl oz) almond milk, 100 ml (3½ fl oz) olive oil and 1 tablespoon cider vinegar together in a jug. Add to the dry ingredients and lightly stir together until just mixed. Quickly fold in 2 peeled and coarsely grated carrots, then spoon the mixture into the paper cases or muffin holes and bake in a preheated oven, 190°C (375°F), Gas mark 5, for 15–20 minutes until well risen and golden. Transfer to a wire rack to cool.

potato bread with tomatoes

Serves **4**

Preparation time **30 minutes**,
  plus proving and cooling

Cooking time about **1 hour**

375 g (12 oz) **potato**, peeled
  and cut into chunks
1 teaspoon **fast-action dried
  yeast**
1 teaspoon **caster sugar**
1 tablespoon **sunflower oil**,
  plus extra for oiling
200 g (7 oz) **strong white
  bread flour**, plus extra for
  dusting
100 g (3½ oz) **strong
  wholemeal bread flour**
2 tablespoons chopped
  rosemary
1 tablespoon **thyme leaves**
salt and **pepper**

Topping

2 tablespoons **olive oil**
250 g (8 oz) mixed-coloured
  baby tomatoes, halved
½ teaspoon **thyme leaves**
½ teaspoon **sea salt flakes**

Cook the potato in a large saucepan of lightly salted boiling water for 15–20 minutes until tender but not flaky. Drain really well, reserving the cooking liquid.

Put 6 tablespoons of the cooking liquid into a large bowl and leave to cool until lukewarm. Sprinkle over the yeast, then stir in the sugar and set aside for 10 minutes.

Mash the potatoes with the oil, then stir in the yeast mixture and mix well with a wooden spoon. Mix in the flours, herbs and salt and pepper, then turn out on to a lightly floured surface and knead well to incorporate the last of the flour. Knead the dough until soft and pliable, then put in a lightly oiled bowl, cover with clingfilm and leave to rise in a warm place for 1 hour until well risen.

Knead the dough on a lightly floured surface, then roughly shape into a round, place on a baking sheet and lightly cover with oiled clingfilm. Leave to prove in a warm place for 30 minutes. Score a cross into the dough with a knife and bake in a preheated oven, 220°C (425°F), Gas Mark 7, for 35–40 minutes until well risen and crusty on top. Transfer to a wire rack to cool for 30 minutes.

Cut 4 slices of the bread and lightly toast. Meanwhile, heat the oil for the topping in a frying pan, add the tomatoes and cook over a high heat for 2–3 minutes until softened. Stir in the thyme and salt flakes. Serve with the toasted bread, seasoned with pepper.

For sweet potato & onion seed bread, prepare the dough as above, using 375 g (12 oz) sweet potato, peeled and chopped, in place of the potato and boiling for 8–10 minutes until just tender, and 2 tablespoons onion seeds instead of the herbs. Bake as above.

almond, raspberry & date bars

Makes **12**
Preparation time **10 minutes**
Cooking time **15 minutes**

5 tablespoons **crunchy almond butter**
8 tablespoons **agave syrup**
50 g (2 oz) **soya margarine**
4 tablespoons **demerara sugar**
150 g (5 oz) **rolled oats**
2 tablespoons **rice flour**
½ teaspoon **ground cinnamon**
150 g (5 oz) fresh **Medjool dates**, stoned and chopped
110 g (4 oz) **raspberries**
25 g (1 oz) **walnuts**, roughly chopped
1 teaspoon **sesame seeds**
1 tablespoon **sunflower seeds**
sunflower oil, for oiling

Heat the almond butter, agave syrup, vegan margarine and demerara sugar in a saucepan over a very low heat, stirring constantly, until melted. Add the oats, flour, cinnamon and dates and mix well.

Transfer the mixture to a lightly oiled 18 x 28 cm (7 x 11 inch) shallow baking tin and level with the back of a metal spoon, slightly dampened to ease spreading. With a teaspoon, make holes in the mixture and press in the raspberries, then scatter with the walnuts, sesame seeds and sunflower seeds. Bake in a preheated oven, 190°C (375°F), Gas Mark 5, for 15 minutes, or until the edges turn a pale golden brown.

Leave to cool in the tin for 10 minutes before scoring into 12 bars, then leave to cool completely before cutting into bars and carefully removing from the tin.

For peanut butter, banana & raisin oat bars,
prepare the mixture as above, replacing the almond butter with 6 tablespoons crunchy peanut butter and using 1 large banana, finely chopped, instead of the dates. Stir 4 tablespoons jumbo raisins into the mixture before baking and then cooling, scoring and cutting into squares as above.

plum, banana & apple crumbles

Serves **4**

Preparation time **15 minutes**

Cooking time **30 minutes**

6 **plums**, halved and stoned

50 g (2 oz) **vegan margarine**

2 **dessert apples**, peeled, cored and cut into chunks

2 tablespoons **demerara sugar**

2 **bananas**, cut into chunks

½ teaspoon **ground cinnamon**

pinch of **ground allspice** (optional)

Crumble

100 g (3½ oz) **plain flour**

50 g (2 oz) **vegan margarine**, cubed

4 tablespoons **demerara sugar**

4 tablespoons **rolled oats**

Cook the plums with the vegan margarine in a saucepan over a gentle heat for 3 minutes. Add the apples and demerara sugar and cook, stirring occasionally, for a further 2–3 minutes.

Remove the pan from the heat, add the bananas and spices and toss gently to lightly coat all the fruit in the sugar and spice. Divide the mixture between 4 x 250 ml (8 fl oz) gratin dishes.

Put the flour for the crumble in a bowl, add the spread and rub in with the fingertips until the mixture resembles fine breadcrumbs. Stir in the sugar and oats. Spoon evenly over the top of the fruit in each dish, place the dishes on a baking sheet and then bake in a preheated oven, 200°C (400°F), Gas Mark 6, for 20 minutes until the crumble is golden and the fruit is bubbling. Serve with natural soya yogurt if liked.

For prune & banana crumbles, put 250 g (8 oz) ready-to-eat pitted prunes into a saucepan with 1 tablespoon demerara, ½ teaspoon ground cinnamon and 150 ml (¼ pint) water. Bring to the boil, then cover and simmer for 3 minutes. Remove from the heat and stir in 2 sliced bananas. Divide between the dishes, top with the crumble mixture and bake as above. Serve with natural soya yogurt.

home-baked beans on toast

Serves **4**

Preparation time **10 minutes**,
  plus overnight soaking

Cooking time
  1 hour 20 minutes

350 g (11½ oz) **dried haricot
  beans**

2 tablespoons **rapeseed oil**

1 **red onion**, cut into wedges

400 g (13 oz) can **chopped
  tomatoes**

2 tablespoons **tomato purée**

2 tablespoons **dark
  muscovado sugar**

3 tablespoons **red wine
  vinegar**

1 teaspoon **paprika**

1 teaspoon **mustard powder**

275 ml (9 fl oz) **vegetable
  stock**

salt and **pepper**

2 tablespoons chopped
  flat leaf parsley, to garnish

wholemeal toast, to serve

Soak the beans in plenty of cold water overnight. Drain, tip into a saucepan and cover with cold water. Bring to the boil, then drain and return to the pan. Cover with fresh cold water, bring to the boil and boil for 10 minutes, then cover and simmer for 50 minutes until tender.

Meanwhile, heat the oil in a separate saucepan, add the onion and fry for 3 minutes until just starting to soften. Add the tomatoes, tomato purée, sugar, vinegar, paprika, mustard powder and stock. Bring to the boil, stirring, then reduce the heat and simmer, uncovered, for 20 minutes until reduced slightly.

Drain the cooked beans and add to the tomato sauce. Simmer for a further 15–20 minutes, covered, until thick, then season with salt and pepper and serve on wholemeal toast, scattered with the chopped parsley.

For quick chilli beans with vegetable sausages,
heat a 400 g (13 oz) can chopped tomatoes in a saucepan with 2 tablespoons each tomato purée and dark muscovado sugar, 1 tablespoon sweet chilli sauce and 1 chopped red chilli. Bring to the boil, stirring, then simmer, uncovered, for 10 minutes. Add a drained 400 g (13 oz) can haricot beans and simmer for a further 10 minutes. Meanwhile, grill or fry 300 g (10 oz) vegan vegetable sausages. Cut into chunks and stir into the bean mixture. Serve on wholemeal toast.

cranberry, oat & raisin cookies

Makes **12**
Preparation time **10 minutes**
Cooking time **12–15 minutes**

50 g (2 oz) **soya margarine** or
   other vegan spread
6 tablespoons **golden syrup**
125 g (4 oz) **wholemeal plain
   flour**
75 g (3 oz) **rolled oats**
1 teaspoon **baking powder**
½ teaspoon **ground
   cinnamon**
½ teaspoon **ground ginger**
pinch of freshly grated **nutmeg**
50 g (2 oz) **dried cranberries**
50 g (2 oz) **raisins**

Heat the spread with the syrup in a saucepan over a low heat, stirring, until melted. Remove from the heat, add the remaining ingredients and mix well.

Spoon the mixture on to a large baking sheet lined with baking parchment into 12 large mounds and press down slightly with the back of a spoon. Bake in a preheated oven, 180°C (350°F), Gas Mark 4, for 8–10 minutes until the edges are golden but the centres are still soft.

Leave to cool for 2–3 minutes on the baking sheet before transferring to a wire rack to cool completely.

For chocolate & cherry cookies, melt the spread with the golden syrup, then remove from the heat, add the flour and rolled oats and mix well as above. Leave to cool for 10 minutes, then stir in 75 g (3 oz) roughly chopped plain dark chocolate (90 per cent cocoa solids) and 50 g (2 oz) dried cherries. Form into 12 mounds and bake as above.

creamy mushrooms with walnuts

Serves **2**

Preparation time **10 minutes**

Cooking time **8 minutes**

1 tablespoon **olive oil**

150 g (5 oz) **chestnut mushrooms**, trimmed and sliced

1 **garlic clove**, crushed

2 **thyme sprigs**, plus extra to garnish

150 ml (1 ¼ pint) **soya** or **oat cream**

1 teaspoon **soy sauce**

50 g (2 oz) **chopped walnuts**, toasted

pepper

bagels, halved and toasted

Heat the oil in a frying pan, add the mushrooms and cook over a high heat, stirring frequently, for 2 minutes until browned and softened.

Reduce the heat and add the garlic, thyme, soya or oat cream and soy sauce. Simmer, stirring, for 3 minutes, adding a little water if the sauce is too thick. Stir in the walnuts and season with pepper (the soy sauce is salty, so you won't need to season with salt).

Spoon the mushroom mixture over the toasted bagels and garnish with thyme sprigs before serving.

For creamy kale with sun-dried tomatoes, heat 1 tablespoon olive oil in a frying pan, add 1 crushed garlic clove and 200 g (7 oz) shredded kale and cook over a medium-high heat, stirring, for 5 minutes until the kale is just tender. Add 150 ml (¼ pint) coconut cream and 1 teaspoon soy sauce and simmer, stirring, for 2 minutes, adding a little water if the sauce is too thick. Stir in 50 g (2 oz) chopped drained sun-dried tomatoes in oil and season with pepper. Heat for 1 minute, then spoon over halved and toasted bagels to serve.

starters, snacks & soups

tapenade bruschetta

Makes **12**

Preparation time **15 minutes**

Cooking time **10 minutes**

1 small **ciabatta loaf**, cut into
12 slices

3 tablespoons **olive oil**

1 **garlic clove**, crushed

1 tablespoon chopped
flat leaf parsley

12 **marinated sun-dried
tomatoes in oil**, drained

Tapenade

150 g (5 oz) **pitted black
olives**

1 **garlic clove**

small handful of **flat leaf
parsley**

2 tablespoons **capers**

1 tablespoon **lemon juice**

2 tablespoons **olive oil**

salt and **pepper**

Arrange the ciabatta slices in a single layer on a baking sheet. Mix the oil, garlic and chopped parsley together and brush over the bread slices. Bake in a preheated oven, 200°C (400°F), Gas Mark 6, for 10 minutes until golden and crisp.

Meanwhile, put the olives, garlic, parsley, capers, lemon juice and oil in a food processor and process to a coarse paste. Season with salt and pepper.

Spread the tapenade over the toasts and top each with a sun-dried tomato.

For artichoke tapenade bruschetta, toast the ciabatta slices as above. Meanwhile, put 75 g (3 oz) each pitted green olives and drained marinated artichokes in oil (reserving 2 tablespoons of the oil), small handful of flat leaf parsley, 2 tablespoons capers, 1 garlic clove, 1 tablespoon lemon juice and the reserved artichoke oil in a food processor and process to a coarse paste. Season with salt and pepper. Spread the tapenade over the toasts and sprinkle with chopped parsley.

summer vegetable tempura

Serves **4**
Preparation time **20 minutes**
Cooking time **15 minutes**

vegetable oil, for deep-frying
75 g (3 oz) **plain flour**
2 tablespoons **cornflour**
pinch of **salt**
200 ml (7 fl oz) ice-cold
  sparkling water
1 **red pepper**, cored,
  deseeded and cut into strips
150 g (5 oz) thin **asparagus
  spears**, trimmed
1 **courgette**, trimmed and
  sliced

Dipping sauce
2 tablespoons **sweet chilli
  sauce**
2 tablespoons **soy sauce**
1 teaspoon finely grated
  lemon rind
1 tablespoon **lemon juice**

Mix the dipping sauce ingredients together in a serving bowl and set aside.

Half-fill a deep saucepan with vegetable oil and heat to 180–190°C (350–375°F), or until a cube of bread dropped into the oil browns in 30 seconds. Just before the oil is hot enough, using a hand whisk, quickly beat the flour, cornflour, salt and sparkling water together in a bowl to make a slightly lumpy batter.

Dip one-third of the vegetables into the batter until coated and then drop straight into the hot oil. Fry for 2 minutes until crisp. Remove from the pan with a slotted spoon, drain on kitchen paper and keep warm in a low oven.

Fry the remaining vegetables in 2 more batches. Serve hot with the dipping sauce.

For broccoli & mushroom tempura with sesame dipping sauce, mix together 3 tablespoons soy sauce, 1 tablespoon sesame oil, the juice of 1 lime and 1 finely chopped spring onion in a serving bowl for a dipping sauce and set aside. Make the batter as above. Dip 250 g (8 oz) broccoli florets and 175 g (6 oz) button mushrooms, trimmed, into the batter to coat and deep-fry, in batches, as above. Serve hot with the sesame dipping sauce..

broad bean & herb crostini

Makes **12**
Preparation time **20 minutes**
Cooking time **15 minutes**

250 g (8 oz) podded **broad beans** (you will need about double this quantity if buying in the pod)
2 tablespoons chopped **mint**
1 tablespoon chopped **flat leaf parsley**
finely grated rind of 1 **lemon**
2 **spring onions**, finely chopped
1 **garlic clove**, crushed
12 slices of **French bread**
2 tablespoons **chilli oil**
salt and **pepper**
rocket, to garnish
lemon wedges, to serve

Cook the broad beans in a saucepan of boiling water for 3 minutes. Drain, rinse under cold water and drain again. Pop the beans out of the outer skins and put in a bowl.

Crush the beans lightly with a potato masher, then stir in the mint, parsley, lemon rind, spring onions and garlic. Season with salt and pepper.

Heat a griddle pan or frying pan until hot. Brush the bread slices with the chilli oil, add to the hot pan, in batches, and cook for 1 minute until toasted and crisp. Turn and cook on the other side for 1 minute.

Spoon the broad bean mixture on to the toasts, garnish with rocket and serve with lemon wedges for squeezing over.

For broad bean, coriander & cumin crostini,

cook the broad beans as above, then peel and place in a bowl. Toast 1 tablespoon cumin seeds in a dry frying pan over a medium heat, shaking the pan occasionally, until starting to smell fragrant and then add to the beans. Lightly crush the beans and cumin together with a potato masher. Stir in 2 tablespoons chopped coriander, ½ finely chopped green chilli and 1 tablespoon lemon juice. Season with salt and pepper. Toast the French bread slices as above, then spoon on the broad bean mixture and garnish with thinly sliced red onion and coriander leaves.

avocado & cucumber sushi

Serves **4**

Preparation time **20 minutes**, plus standing/steaming

Cooking time **15 minutes**

200 g (7 oz) **sushi rice**

4 tablespoons **rice vinegar**

2 tablespoons **granulated sugar**

2 tablespoons **sesame seeds**, toasted

4 sheets of **nori seaweed**

1 small **avocado**, peeled, stoned and cut into slim wedges

¼ **cucumber**, cut into long thin sticks

To serve

soy sauce

wasabi

pickled ginger

Cook and leave the rice to stand/steam according to the packet instructions, then transfer to a bowl.

Put the vinegar and sugar in a cup and microwave for 30 seconds until hot. Pour into the cooked rice and mix well – the rice should be sticky. Stir in the sesame seeds.

Lay out the sheets of nori seaweed and divide the rice between them. Spread evenly to the edges, then arrange the avocado wedges and cucumber strips across the length of the rice in the bottom third of each sheet. Starting at the filled end, gently roll the each nori sheet up tightly until a neat roll is formed, brushing with a little water to hold the seaweed tightly in place.

Use a very sharp knife to slice the rolls into 2.5 cm (1 inch) thick pieces. Serve with soy sauce and wasabi for dipping, along with some pickled ginger.

For asparagus & red pepper rolls, cook 8 trimmed asparagus spears and ½ red pepper, cored, deseeded and cut into strips, in a saucepan of salted boiling water for 2 minutes until just tender, then immediately remove with a slotted spoon to a colander, rinse with cold water and drain. Set aside on kitchen paper to cool. Cook and leave the sushi rice to stand/steam as above, then use the asparagus and red pepper in place of the avocado and cucumber to prepare 4 nori rolls as above. Slice and serve as above.

aubergine dip & crispy tortillas

Serves **6**

Preparation time **15 minutes**, plus cooling

Cooking time **30 minutes**

1 large **aubergine**, about 750 g (1½ lb), trimmed and cut into thick chunks

8 tablespoons **extra virgin olive oil**

1 **garlic clove**, crushed

½ teaspoon **smoked paprika**

3 tablespoons **tahini**

juice of 1 **lemon**

1 tablespoon chopped **flat leaf parsley**

salt and **pepper**

Tortillas

6 mini **flour tortillas**, cut into triangles

1 tablespoon **olive oil**

1 teaspoon **sea salt flakes**

Put the aubergine in a bowl with 6 tablespoons of the extra virgin olive oil and toss well. Transfer to a large roasting tin and roast in a preheated oven, 220°C (425°F), Gas Mark 7, for 25 minutes until soft and lightly charred in places. Leave to cool.

Transfer the aubergine to a food processor and add the garlic, ¼ teaspoon of the smoked paprika, the tahini, lemon juice, half the chopped parsley and plenty of salt and pepper. Process until smooth, then transfer to a serving bowl.

Mix the remaining extra virgin olive oil with the remaining paprika and use to swirl over the top of the dip. Scatter with the remaining chopped parsley.

Brush each tortilla triangle lightly with the olive oil and spread out on 1–2 large baking sheets. Sprinkle with the salt and cook under a preheated medium grill for 1–2 minutes until lightly crisp and golden. Arrange around the bowl of dip and serve.

For spicy chilli, aubergine & red pepper dip, toss a 450 g (14½ oz) aubergine, trimmed and cut into chunks, and 1 large red pepper, cored, deseeded and cut into chunks, with 6 tablespoons extra virgin olive oil. Transfer to a roasting tin and roast in a preheated oven, 220°C (425°F), Gas Mark 7 for 25 minutes until soft and lightly charred. Leave to cool, then transfer to a food processor with ½ deseeded and finely chopped red chilli, 4 tablespoons chopped coriander, a pinch of salt and plenty of pepper and process until smooth. Transfer to a serving bowl, scatter with chopped coriander and serve with crispy tortillas, prepared as above.

flatbread, roasted veg & hummus

Serves **4**

Preparation time **20 minutes**, plus standing

Cooking time **20 minutes**

200 g (7 oz) **wholemeal plain flour**, plus extra for dusting

½ teaspoon **salt**

1 **red pepper**, cored, deseeded and cut into chunks

1 **orange pepper**, cored, deseeded and cut into chunks

1 **green pepper**, cored, deseeded and cut into chunks

1 large **red onion**, cut into slim wedges

2 tablespoons **olive oil**

½ teaspoon **ground coriander**

½ teaspoon **cumin seeds**

Hummus

400 g (13 oz) can **chickpeas**, drained well

finely grated rind and juice of 1 **lemon**

3 tablespoons chopped **parsley**

1 tablespoon **tahini**

3 tablespoons **olive oil**

salt and **pepper**

Mix the flour and salt together in a bowl, then add enough water to bring the mixture together into a dough – about 7–8 tablespoons. Turn out on to a lightly floured surface and knead well until smooth. Return to the bowl, cover with clingfilm and leave in a warm place for 30 minutes.

Toss the peppers and onion with the oil in a large roasting tin, then add the coriander and cumin and toss again. Roast in a preheated oven, 220°C (425°F), Gas Mark 7, for 20 minutes until softened.

Meanwhile, blend together all the ingredients for the hummus in a blender or food processor until smooth.

Divide the flatbread dough into 4 pieces and roll out each into a 25 cm (10 inch) round. Heat a large frying pan until hot and cook the flatbreads for about 45 seconds on each side until lightly golden, flipping over with a fish slice.

Spread each warm flatbread with some of the hummus, then top with one-quarter of the hot roasted vegetables and fold to serve.

For seeded flatbreads with roasted veg & butter bean paste, prepare the flatbread dough as above, mixing 1 tablespoon cumin seeds with the flour and salt. Roast the vegetables as above, omitting the cumin seeds. Blend together a well-drained 400 g (13 oz) can butter beans, 3 tablespoons olive oil, 1 tablespoon thyme leaves, finely grated rind of 1 lemon, 1 crushed garlic clove and salt and pepper in a blender until smooth. Cook the flatbread dough and then serve rolled up with the bean paste and roasted veg as above.

mushroom risotto cakes

Serves **4**

Preparation time **20 minutes**, plus cooling

Cooking time **25 minutes**

3 tablespoons **olive oil**

1 **red onion**, finely chopped

1 **leek**, trimmed, cleaned and very finely sliced

250 g (8 oz) **chestnut mushrooms**, trimmed and roughly chopped

1 **garlic clove**, crushed

200 g (7 oz) **Arborio rice**

600 ml (1 pint) **vegetable stock**, plus extra if needed

150 ml (¼ pint) **white wine**

75 g (3 oz) **cornmeal**

4 tablespoons **sunflower oil**

Heat the olive oil in a large, heavy-based frying pan, add the onion, leek, mushrooms, and garlic and cook over a medium-high heat for 5–6 minutes until softened and golden in places. Add the rice and stir well, then add the stock and wine, reduce the heat to a gentle simmer and cook, stirring frequently, until the liquid is almost all absorbed and the rice is tender and cooked through, adding more stock if necessary.

Remove the pan from the heat and leave to cool for 20 minutes. The mixture will not only cool but more liquid will be absorbed and the rice will become a little more stodgy.

Divide the mixture into 8 and mould each portion into a large patty, then toss liberally in the cornmeal and set aside.

Heat the sunflower oil in a frying pan and cook the cakes over a medium-high heat for 2–3 minutes on each side until golden and crisp. Serve hot with a simple dressed salad.

For butternut squash risotto cakes, cook the onion and leek over a medium-high heat as above with 200 g (7 oz) peeled, deseeded and finely chopped butternut squash pieces in place of the mushrooms. Then reduce the heat, cover and cook for a further 3–4 minutes. Remove the lid, add the rice and continue as above. Serve the cakes with a simple salad.

seeded chips with red pepper dip

Serves **4**

Preparation time **20 minutes**

Cooking time **35 minutes**

450 g (14½ oz) **sweet potatoes**, peeled and cut into wedges

450 g (14½ oz) **white potatoes**, peeled and cut into wedges

4 tablespoons **olive oil**

1 tablespoon **poppy seeds**

1 tablespoon **sesame seeds**

1 teaspoon **dried chilli flakes**

1 large **red pepper**, cored, deseeded and cut into 4 wedges

2 **tomatoes**, halved

½ teaspoon **smoked paprika**

3 tablespoons **chopped coriander**

salt and **pepper**

Drizzle the sweet potato and white potato wedges with 3 tablespoons of the olive oil in a large roasting tin and toss well, then scatter over the poppy and sesame seeds and chilli flakes and toss again. Season generously with salt and pepper and roast in the top of a preheated oven, 200°C (400°F), Gas Mark 6, for 35 minutes until golden.

Meanwhile, put the pepper wedges and tomatoes in a smaller roasting tin, then drizzle with the remaining olive oil and toss well. Roast on a lower shelf in the oven for 25 minutes until softened and lightly charred in places.

Transfer the roasted pepper and tomatoes to a food processor, season generously with salt and pepper and add the smoked paprika. Process until almost smooth but with a little texture still remaining. Spoon into a small serving bowl and place in the centre of a serving platter.

Arrange the roasted potato wedges on the platter, scatter with the chopped coriander and serve.

For parsnip chips with horseradish dip, peel

4 large parsnips, cut each into 8 wedges and put in a roasting tin. Toss with 3 tablespoons olive oil and roast in a preheated oven, 200°C (400°F), Gas Mark 6, for 25 minutes until softened and crisp at the edges. Toss with 2 tablespoons maple syrup and 1 tablespoon wholegrain mustard, then arrange on a serving platter and serve with a bowl of horseradish sauce for dipping.

aubergine with caper & mint pesto

Serves **4**
Preparation time **20 minutes**
Cooking time **15 minutes**

2 **aubergines**, trimmed and
   sliced
150 ml (¼ pint) **extra virgin
   olive oil**
warm **pitta bread,** to serve

Pesto
finely grated rind and juice of
   1 **lemon**
3 tablespoons **olive oil**
2 tablespoons **red wine
   vinegar**
4 tablespoons chopped **mint
   leaves**, plus extra leaves to
   garnish
2 tablespoons **capers**, roughly
   chopped
1 **garlic clove**, roughly
   chopped
1 teaspooon **sugar**
salt and **pepper**

Put the aubergine slices in a large bowl, pour over the
oil and toss well, using both hands to coat as evenly
as possible. The oil will be absorbed fast, so work as
quickly as possible. Set aside for 10 minutes while
making the pesto.

Mix all the pesto ingredients together in a jug. Season
with a little salt and pepper.

Heat a griddle pan until smoking, then lay several of
the aubergine slices on to the hot pan in a single layer
and cook over a high heat for 1–2 minutes on each
side until lightly charred and soft. Transfer to heatproof
platter and keep warm in a low oven while cooking the
remaining slices.

Drizzle or spoon some of the pesto over the aubergine
slices and serve with warm pitta bread, with the
remaining pesto separately.

For warm griddled vegetables with classic pesto,
cut 2 red peppers into quarters, discarding the cores
and seeds, and put in a large bowl. Add 2 courgettes,
trimmed and sliced lengthways, and 4 large mushrooms,
trimmed, then pour over 6 tablespoons olive oil and toss
well. To make the pesto, mix together 4 tablespoons
chopped basil, 3 tablespoons olive oil and 2 tablespoons
each red wine vinegar and lightly toasted pine nuts,
roughly chopped, in a jug. Season generously with salt
and pepper. Heat a griddle pan until smoking, add the
vegetables, in batches, and cook over a high heat for
2–3 minutes on each side until lightly charred and soft.
Arrange on a serving platter and drizzle with the pesto
to serve.

tomato & thyme tart

Serves **6**
Preparation time **20 minutes**, plus chilling
Cooking time **35 minutes**

250 g (8 oz) **plain flour**, plus extra for dusting
125 g (4 oz) **soya spread**, cubed
4 tablespoons **thyme leaves**, plus extra for garnish
2–3 tablespoons **cold water**
3 tablespoons **olive oil**
1 **onion**, finely chopped
250 g (8 oz) mixed-coloured **cherry tomatoes**, halved
½ teaspoon **sea salt flakes**
salt and **pepper**

Put the flour in a bowl and season with salt and pepper. Add the spread and rub in with the fingertips until the mixture resembles fine breadcrumbs. Stir in half the thyme, then add enough of the measurement water to bring the mixture together into a firm dough.

Roll the dough out on a lightly floured surface and use to line a 23 cm (9 inch) fluted flan tin. Chill until ready to use.

Heat 1 tablespoon of the oil in a frying pan, add the onion and cook over a medium-high heat for 5–6 minutes until softened and golden. Stir in the remaining thyme leaves and cook for a further 1 minute. Spoon the onion mixture into the pastry case and smooth over.

Toss the tomatoes in a bowl with the remaining oil, salt flakes and plenty of pepper. Arrange on top of the onion in the pastry case and bake in a preheated oven, 220°C (425°F), Gas Mark 7, for 20–25 minutes until the pastry is golden and the tomatoes softened and lightly charred in places. Garnish with thyme leaves to serve.

For mixed tomato calzone, make up a 250 g (8 oz) packet pizza base mix according to the instructions and set aside. Heat 1 tablespoon olive oil in a frying pan, add 1 roughly chopped onion and cook over a medium-high heat for 5–6 minutes until softened and golden. Toss in a bowl with 175 g (6 oz) cherry tomatoes, halved, and 1 tablespoon thyme leaves. Roll out the pizza base mix on a lightly floured surface into a 25 cm (10 inch) round and pile the tomato mixture on to one half. Lightly brush the edges with cold water and fold over to seal. Place on a baking sheet and bake in a preheated oven, 220°C (425°F), Gas Mark 7, for 20 minutes until golden.

pea & pesto soup

Serves **4**
Preparation time **15 minutes**
Cooking time **25 minutes**

1 tablespoon **olive oil**
1 **leek**, trimmed, cleaned and chopped
1 **potato**, peeled and chopped
575 ml (18 fl oz) **vegetable stock**
350 g (11½ oz) **frozen peas**
salt
ciabatta croûtons, to serve

Pesto
50 g (2 oz) **pine nuts**, toasted
2 large handfuls of **basil leaves**, plus extra to garnish
1 **garlic clove**
50 g (2 oz) Parmesan-style or mature Cheddar-style **vegan cheese**
100 ml (3½ fl oz) **olive oil**
salt and **pepper**

Process the pine nuts, basil, garlic and vegan cheese for the pesto in a food processor until finely chopped. With the motor running, gradually add the oil until blended. Season with salt and pepper. Set aside.

Heat the oil in a saucepan, add the leek and potato and cook over a gentle heat for 5 minutes until softened. Add the stock and bring to the boil, then cover and simmer for 10 minutes. Stir in the peas and cook for a further 5 minutes, then stir in 4 tablespoons of the pesto.

Transfer the soup in batches to the food processor or a blender and blend until smooth. Return to the pan and reheat, then season with salt and add more pesto, if liked, to taste (the remainder will keep in the refrigerator for several days). Ladle into bowls, spoon over any remaining pesto, garnish with basil leaves and serve with ciabatta croûtons.

For courgette soup with pesto, prepare the pesto as above (or use shop-bought vegan pesto). Heat the oil in a saucepan and add the leek and potato as above with 1 trimmed and chopped courgette and 1 crushed garlic clove, then cook over a gentle heat for 5 minutes until softened. Add the stock as above and bring to the boil, then cover and simmer for 15 minutes. Stir in 4 tablespoons pesto and then blend the soup in batches in a food processor or blender until smooth. Reheat, season with salt and pepper and add more pesto, if liked, to taste. Garnish with basil leaves and serve with ciabatta croûtons.

black bean soup with noodles

Serves **4**
Preparation time **10 minutes**
Cooking time **10 minutes**

2 tablespoons **groundnut** or
  vegetable oil
bunch of **spring onions**, sliced
2 **garlic cloves**, roughly
  chopped
1 **red chilli,** deseeded and
  sliced
3.5 cm (1 ½ inch) piece of
  fresh root ginger, peeled
  and grated
125 ml (4 fl oz) **black bean
  sauce** or **black bean stir-fry
  sauce**
750 ml (1 ¼ pints) **vegetable
  stock**
200 g (7 oz) **pak choi** or
  spring greens, shredded
2 teaspoons **soy sauce**
1 teaspoon **caster sugar**
50 g (2 oz) **raw unsalted
  peanuts**
200 g (7 oz) **dried Japanese
  soba noodles**

Heat the oil in a saucepan, add the spring onions and
garlic and cook gently for 1 minute.

Add the chilli, ginger, black bean sauce and stock and
bring to the boil. Stir in the pak choi or spring greens,
soy sauce, sugar and peanuts, then simmer gently,
uncovered, for 4 minutes.

Meanwhile, cook the noodles in a saucepan of boiling
water for about 5 minutes, or until just tender.

Drain the noodles and pile into serving bowls. Ladle the
soup over the noodles and serve immediately.

For black bean soba nests, cook 200 g (7 oz) dried
Japanese soba noodles as above, drain and set aside.
Meanwhile, heat 1 tablespoon vegetable oil in a wok or
large frying pan, add a bunch of spring onions, roughly
but chunkily chopped, and 1 thinly sliced red chilli and
stir-fry over a medium-high heat for 1 minute. Add
a 2.5 cm (1 inch) piece of fresh root ginger, peeled
and roughly chopped, and 1 head of pak choi, roughly
sliced, and stir-fry for 1 minute. Add 150 ml (¼ pint)
black bean sauce or black bean stir-fry sauce and heat
through until piping hot. Remove from the heat and toss
in the cooked noodles. Using 2 forks, twist the noodles
into 8 nests and place 2 nests on each of 4 small
serving plates, then scatter with 3 tablespoons roughly
chopped peanuts and 1 tablespoon chopped coriander.
Serve as a starter.

roasted red pepper & lentil soup

Serves **4**

Preparation time **20 minutes**

Cooking time **45 minutes**

2 **red peppers**, quartered,
cored and deseeded

1 **red onion**, cut into wedges

1 tablespoon **olive oil**

3 **garlic cloves**, unpeeled

200 g (7 oz) **dried red split
lentils**, rinsed and drained

1 teaspoon **dried chilli flakes**

1 teaspoon **ground cumin**

1 litre (1¾ pint) **vegetable
stock**

2 tablespoons **mixed seeds**,
such as pumpkin, sunflower,
sesame and flaxseed
(linseed), toasted

salt and **pepper**

roughly chopped **coriander**,
to garnish

Put the peppers and onion on a baking sheet. Drizzle over the oil, season with salt and pepper and toss until evenly coated in the oil, then spread out in a single layer. Roast in a preheated oven, 200°C (400°F), Gas Mark 6, for 20 minutes, turning once and adding the garlic cloves halfway through, until the peppers are starting to char and the onions are soft.

Squeeze the soft garlic out of its skin and place in a saucepan. Add the roasted peppers to the pan with the onion and any oil from the baking sheet. Add the lentils, chilli flakes, cumin and stock and bring to the boil, then cover and simmer for 20 minutes until the lentils are soft.

Transfer the soup in batches to a blender or food processor and blend until smooth. Return to the pan and reheat through. Ladle into bowls, sprinkle over the toasted seeds and garnish with chopped coriander.

For roasted tomato, lentil & basil soup, spread 1 kg (2 lb) halved tomatoes out in a shallow roasting tin, drizzle with 2 tablespoons olive oil and season with salt and pepper. Roast in a preheated oven, 200°C (400°F), Gas Mark 6, for 10 minutes, then add 3 unpeeled garlic cloves and roast for 10 minutes until soft. Squeeze the soft garlic out of its skin into a saucepan. Add the tomatoes, removing as many of the skins as possible, and any juices from the tin with 200 g (7 oz) rinsed dried red split lentils, 2 tablespoons sun-dried tomato purée, 1 teaspoon dried chilli flakes, a handful of basil leaves and 1 litre (1¾ pint) vegetable stock. Bring to the boil, then cover and simmer for 20 minutes until the lentils are soft. Blend the soup in batches in a blender or food processor until smooth, then reheat, ladle into bowls and garnish with basil leaves.

tomato & balsamic vinegar soup

Serves **6**
Preparation time **25 minutes**
Cooking time **20 minutes**

750 g (1 ½ lb) large **tomatoes**
on the vine
2 tablespoons **olive oil**
1 **onion**, roughly chopped
1 **baking potato**, about 200 g
(7 oz), peeled and diced
2 **garlic cloves**, finely chopped
(optional)
750 ml (1 ¼ pints) **vegetable stock**
1 tablespoon **tomato purée**
1 tablespoon **soft dark brown sugar**
4 teaspoons **balsamic vinegar**
small bunch of **basil**
salt and **pepper**

Cut the tomatoes in half, place them cut-side down in a foil-lined grill pan and drizzle with some of the oil. Grill for 4–5 minutes under a pre-heated grill until the skins have split and blackened.

Meanwhile, heat the remaining oil in a saucepan, add the onion, potato and garlic, if using, and cook for 5 minutes, stirring occasionally until softened and turning golden around the edges.

Remove the skins from the tomatoes and roughly chop the flesh, then add to the onion and potato with any juices from the grill pan, then stir in the stock, tomato purée, sugar and vinegar. Add half the basil, season with salt and pepper and bring to the boil, then cover and simmer for 15 minutes.

Transfer half the soup to a blender or food processor and blend until smooth. Return to the pan with the remainder of the soup and reheat. Season to taste, then ladle into bowls, garnish with the remaining basil leaves and serve with Parmesan-style vegan cheese pastry twists if liked.

spicy coriander & lentil soup

Serves **8**

Preparation time **10–15 minutes**

Cooking time **about 50 minutes**

2 tablespoons **vegetable oil**

2 **onions**, chopped

2 **garlic cloves**, chopped

2 **celery sticks**, chopped

500 g (1 lb) **dried red split lentils**, rinsed and drained

400 g (13 oz) **can tomatoes**, drained

1 **chilli**, deseeded and chopped (optional)

1 teaspoon **paprika**

1 teaspoon **harissa**

1 teaspoon **ground cumin**

1.2 litres (2 pints) **vegetable stock**

salt and **pepper**

2 tablespoons chopped **coriander**, to garnish

Heat the oil in a large saucepan, add the onions, garlic and celery and cook over a gentle heat for a few minutes until softened.

Stir the lentils into the pan with the tomatoes. Add the chilli, if using, paprika, harissa, cumin and stock and season with salt and pepper.

Bring to the boil, then cover and simmer gently for about 40–50 minutes until the lentils are tender, adding a little more stock or water if the soup gets too thick. Serve garnished with the chopped coriander.

For spicy coriander & white bean soup, cook the onions, garlic and celery in the oil as above. Drain 2 x 425 g (14 oz) cans haricot or cannellini beans, then add to the pan with the chilli, flavourings and stock as above. Simmer for 40–50 minutes, then roughly mash some of the beans to thicken the soup. Stir in 2 tablespoons chopped coriander and 4 tablespoons chopped parsley to finish.

butternut soup with peanut pesto

Serves **6**
Preparation time **20 minutes**
Cooking time **40 minutes**

2 tablespoons **olive oil**
1 **onion**, finely chopped
1 **butternut squash**, about 750 g (1½ lb) peeled, deseeded and cut into chunks
400 g (13 oz) can **coconut milk**
1 tablespoon vegan **Thai green curry paste**
600 ml (1 pint) **vegetable stock**

Pesto
1 **green chilli**, deseeded and finely chopped
2 tablespoons **peanuts**, roughly chopped
4 tablespoons chopped **coriander**
1 cm (½ inch) piece of **fresh root ginger**, peeled and grated
1 tablespoon **olive oil**
salt and **pepper**

Mix all the ingredients for the pesto together in a small serving bowl and season with a little salt and plenty of pepper. Set aside.

Heat the oil in a large, heavy-based saucepan, add the onion and butternut squash and cook over a medium-high heat for 5–6 minutes until softened and golden in places. Add the coconut milk, curry paste and stock and bring to the boil, stirring constantly. Cover and simmer gently for 30 minutes until the squash is tender.

Transfer the soup in batches to a blender or food processor and blend until smooth. Return to the pan and reheat. Ladle into warmed serving bowls, spoon over a little of the pesto and swirl through with a skewer.

For spiced pumpkin soup with extra-hot red chilli pesto, mix together 1 finely chopped red chilli, 4 tablespoons chopped coriander, 1 tablespoon olive oil and ½ teaspoon roughly chopped cumin seeds for the pesto. Heat 3 tablespoons olive oil in a large saucepan, add 750 g (1½ lb) pumpkin, peeled, deseeded and chopped, and 1 chopped onion and cook over a medium-high heat for 5–6 minutes until softened and golden in places. Add ½ finely chopped red chilli and 1 teaspoon each ground cumin and ground coriander and cook for a further 2 minutes, stirring constantly. Add 900 ml (1½ pints) vegetable stock and bring to the boil. Cover and simmer for 20 minutes until the pumpkin is tender. Season with salt and pepper. Blend the soup in batches in a blender or food processor until smooth, then reheat. Ladle into warmed serving bowls and top each with a spoonful of the pesto.

red bean soup cajun-style

Serves **6**
Preparation time **25 minutes**,
  plus overnight soaking
Cooking time **1 hour**

2 tablespoons **sunflower oil**
1 large **onion**, chopped
1 **red pepper**, cored,
  deseeded and diced
1 **carrot**, peeled and diced
1 **baking potato**, peeled and
  diced
2–3 **garlic cloves**, chopped
  (optional)
2 teaspoons **Cajun spice mix**
400 g (13 oz) can **chopped
  tomatoes**
1 tablespoon **soft dark brown
  sugar**
1 litre (1¾ pints) **vegetable
  stock**
425 g (14 oz) can **red kidney
  beans**, drained
50 g (2 oz) **okra**, trimmed and
  sliced
50 g (2 oz) **green beans**,
  trimmed and thinly sliced
salt and **pepper**

Heat the oil in a large frying pan, add the onion and
cook over a medium heat for 5 minutes until softened.
Add the red pepper, carrot, potato and garlic, if using,
and cook for a further 5 minutes. Stir in the spice mix,
tomatoes, sugar, stock and plenty of salt and pepper
and bring to the boil.

Stir the kidney beans into the pan and bring to the
boil, then cover and simmer for 45 minutes until the
vegetables are tender.

Add the green vegetables, re-cover and simmer for
5 minutes until just cooked. Serve with crusty bread.

For Hungarian paprika & red bean soup, make the
soup as above, using 1 teaspoon paprika instead of
the Cajun spice mix. Simmer for 45 minutes. Omitting
the green vegetables, transfer the soup in batches to
a blender or food processor and blend until smooth,
then reheat. Ladle into warmed serving bowls and serve
topped with 2 tablespoons natural soya yogurt sprinkled
with a few caraway seeds.

chilli miso soup

Serves **4**
Preparation time **20 minutes**
Cooking time **10 minutes**

2 tablespoons **miso paste**
1 tablespoon **dark soy sauce**
1.4 litres (2½ pints) **vegetable stock**
150 g (5 oz) **dried thin rice noodles**
2.5 cm (1 inch) piece of **fresh root ginger**, peeled and grated
1 tablespoon **sesame oil**
½ **red bird's eye chilli**, deseeded and finely chopped
175 g (6 oz) **sugar snap peas**, diagonally sliced
2 **shallots**, finely chopped
125 g (4 oz) **baby corn**, roughly sliced
6 tablespoons chopped **coriander**
2 **spring onions**, finely sliced, to garnish

Put the miso paste, soy sauce and stock into a large saucepan and bring to the boil. Reduce the heat, add the noodles and ginger and simmer for 5 minutes.

Meanwhile, heat the oil in a wok or large frying pan, add the chilli, sugar snap peas, shallots and baby corn and stir-fry over a medium-high heat for 5 minutes until softened.

Transfer the vegetable mixture to the pan with the stock and noodles, add the coriander and stir through. Serve in warmed serving bowls, garnished with the spring onions.

For miso soup with ramen peppers & tofu, prepare the miso stock as above, then add 175 g (6 oz) dried ramen noodles in place of the thin rice noodles and simmer for 5 minutes. Heat 1 tablespoon sesame oil in a wok or large frying pan, add 1 red and 1 yellow pepper, cored, deseeded and thinly sliced, with 75 g (3 oz) roughly chopped sugar snap peas and stir-fry over a medium-high heat for 5 minutes until softened. Add 125 g (4 oz) firm tofu, drained, patted dry and cubed, and gently toss for a few seconds, then transfer the mixture to the pan with the stock and noodles. Stir through, then serve ladled into warmed bowls.

chickpea minestrone with rocket

Serves **4**
Preparation time **20 minutes**
Cooking time **30 minutes**

2 tablespoons **olive oil**
1 **red onion**, finely chopped
1 **garlic clove**, sliced
400 g (13 oz) can **chickpeas**,
 drained and rinsed
150 g (5 oz) **green beans**,
 trimmed and diagonally
 sliced
200 g (7 oz) **cherry tomatoes**
900 ml (1½ pints) **vegetable
 stock**
300 ml (½ pint) **tomato juice**
150 g (5 oz) **dried
 wholewheat pasta shapes**
70 g (2¾ oz) bag **wild rocket
 leaves**
6 tablespoons chopped **flat
 leaf parsley**
salt and **pepper**

Heat the oil in a large, deep saucepan, add the onion and cook over a medium-high heat for 3–4 minutes until beginning to soften. Add the garlic and cook, stirring, for 1 minute.

Add the chickpeas, green beans and tomatoes to the pan and stir well, then stir in the stock, tomato juice and pasta. Bring to the boil, then cover and simmer for 15 minutes until the pasta is tender.

Remove the lid and continue to cook for a further 10 minutes, adding three-quarters of the rocket and the parsley just before the end of cooking and stirring through. Season generously with salt and pepper.

Serve in warmed serving bowls with the remaining rocket scattered over to garnish, along with warm crusty wholemeal bread.

For a chilli, tomato & cannellini bean soup, heat 2 tablespoons olive oil in a saucepan, add 1 finely chopped red onion and cook over a medium heat for 5 minutes. Add ½ small red chilli, finely chopped, and cook for 1 minute. Stir in 250 g (8 oz) cherry tomatoes, then add 600 ml (1 pint) vegetable stock, 300 ml (½ pint) tomato juice and a 400 g (13 oz) can cannellini beans, drained and rinsed, and bring to the boil. Cover and simmer for 20 minutes, then add 200 g (7 oz) spinach leaves, roughly chopped, and stir through until wilted. Season with salt and pepper, then serve in warmed serving bowls with chunks of crusty bread.

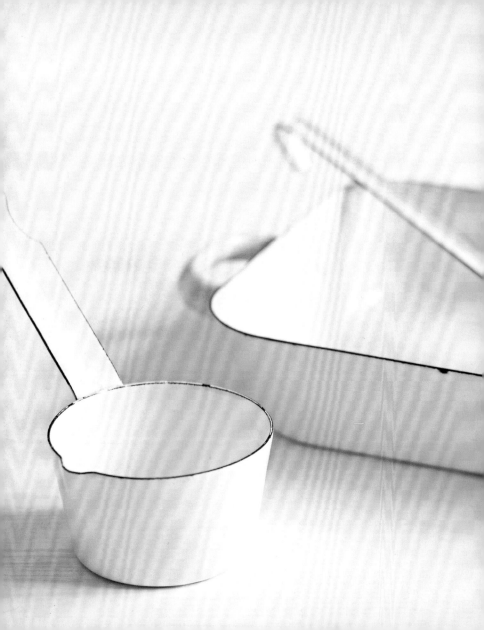

main meals

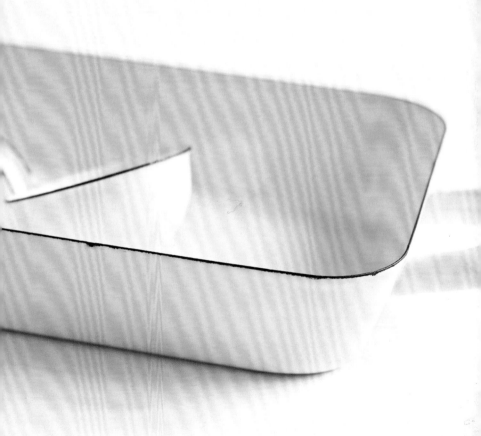

provençale tart

Serves **6**

Preparation time **20 minutes**, plus proving

Cooking time **1 hour**

225 g (7½ oz) **strong white bread flour**, plus extra for dusting

1 teaspoon **salt**

1 teaspoon **caster sugar**

1 teaspoon **fast-action dried yeast**

1 tablespoon **olive oil**

150 ml (¼ pint) **lukewarm water**

Topping

4 tablespoons **olive oil**

1 kg (2 lb) **onions**, sliced

1 **garlic clove**, crushed

1 teaspoon **thyme leaves**, plus extra to garnish

1 teaspoon **dried mixed herbs**

12 **pitted black olives**

12 **cherry tomatoes**, halved

2 tablespoons **capers**

salt and **pepper**

Mix the flour, salt, sugar and yeast together in a bowl. Add the oil and measurement lukewarm water and mix with your hand until the mixture comes together into a dough and leaves the sides of the bowl clean. If too dry, add a little more lukewarm water.

Turn the dough out on to a lightly floured surface and knead for about 10 minutes until smooth and stretchy. Put in a clean bowl, cover with clingfilm and leave to rise in a warm place for about 1 hour until doubled in size.

Meanwhile, make the topping. Heat the oil in a large frying pan, add the onions, garlic, thyme and dried herbs and cook, covered, over a gentle heat, stirring occasionally, for about 30 minutes until the onions are meltingly soft.

Turn the dough out on to a lightly floured surface and knead for 1 minute. Roll out the dough and use to line a 33 x 23 cm (13 x 9 inch) Swiss roll tin. Spread the cooked onions over the top, scatter over the olives, tomatoes and capers and season with salt and pepper. Bake in a preheated oven, 180°C (350°F), Gas Mark 4, for 25 minutes until golden. Garnish with thyme leaves and serve warm or cold.

For tomato tart with basil oil, make the dough and use to line a Swiss roll tin as above. Sprinkle 2 thinly sliced garlic cloves over the dough, topped by 6 thinly sliced tomatoes. Blend a small handful of basil leaves with 3 tablespoons olive oil in a blender and drizzle over the tomatoes. Season with salt and pepper and bake as above. Serve warm.

teriyaki mushrooms & noodles

Serves **4**
Preparation time **10 minutes**
Cooking time **10 minutes**

1 tablespoon **rapeseed oil**
350 g (11½ oz) **assorted mushrooms, such as shitake, open cup and oyster**, trimmed and halved if large
4 tablespoons **mirin** or **dry sherry**
4 tablespoons **soy sauce**
1 tablespoon **light muscovado sugar**
1.5 cm (¾ inch) piece of **fresh root ginger**, peeled and grated
1 teaspoon **sesame oil**
300 g (10 oz) **dried wide rice noodles**
200 g (7 oz) **sugar snap peas**
8 tablespoons **sweet chilli sauce**

Heat the rapeseed oil in a wok or large frying pan, add the mushrooms and stir-fry over a high heat for 3 minutes until browned and tender.

Mix together the mirin or sherry, soy sauce, sugar, ginger and sesame oil in a jug and add to the pan. Cook, stirring occasionally, for 3–4 minutes until the sauce has reduced slightly and coats the mushrooms.

Meanwhile, cook the rice noodles and sugar snap peas in a saucepan of boiling water for 2 minutes, or until the noodles are tender and the sugar snap peas still have a crunch to them. Drain and return to the pan, then add the sweet chilli sauce and toss to lightly coat.

Divide the noodles and sugar snap peas between 4 bowls and spoon the mushrooms and sauce over the top.

For teriyaki tofu with cashew nuts, mix together 4 tablespoons each mirin or dry sherry and soy sauce, 1 tablespoon light muscovado sugar, 1.5 cm (¾ inch) piece of fresh root ginger, peeled and grated, and 1 teaspoon sesame oil in a bowl. Add 350 g (11½ oz) firm tofu, drained, patted dry and cubed, and turn to coat in the sauce, then leave to marinate for 5 minutes. Heat 1 tablespoon rapeseed oil in a wok or large frying pan, add the tofu, removing from the marinade with a slotted spoon, and stir-fry over a high heat for 1 minute, trying not to break up the tofu too much. Pour in the remaining marinade and cook for a further minute. Serve with rice noodles sprinkled with 1 finely chopped red chilli and 50 g (2 oz) chopped toasted cashew nuts.

saffron-scented vegetable tagine

Serves **4**
Preparation time **15 minutes**
Cooking time **50 minutes**

100 ml (3½ fl oz) **sunflower oil**

1 large **onion**, finely chopped

2 **garlic cloves**, finely chopped

2 teaspoons **ground coriander**

2 teaspoons **ground cumin**

2 teaspoons **ground cinnamon**

400 g (13 oz) can **chickpeas**, drained

400 g (13 oz) can **chopped tomatoes**

600 ml (1 pint) **vegetable stock**

¼ teaspoon **saffron threads**

1 large **aubergine**, trimmed and chopped

250 g (8 oz) **button mushrooms**, trimmed and halved if large

100 g (3½ oz) **dried figs**, chopped

2 tablespoons chopped **fresh coriander**

salt and **pepper**

Heat 2 tablespoons of the oil in a frying pan, add the onion, garlic and spices and cook over a medium heat, stirring frequently, for about 5 minutes until the onion is golden.

Transfer the onion mixture to a saucepan with a slotted spoon and add the chickpeas, tomatoes, stock and saffron. Season with salt and pepper.

Heat the remaining oil in the frying pan, add the aubergine and cook over a high heat, stirring frequently, for about 5 minutes until browned. Add to the chickpea mixture and bring to the boil, then cover and simmer gently for 20 minutes.

Stir in the mushrooms and figs and simmer gently, uncovered, for a further 20 minutes. Stir in the chopped coriander and season with salt and pepper. Serve with steamed wholewheat couscous.

For winter vegetable & lentil tagine, cook the onion, garlic and spices as above, then transfer to a saucepan and add a drained 400 g (13 oz) can green lentils in place of the chickpeas, along with the tomatoes, stock and saffron. Instead of the aubergine, cook 2 peeled and sliced carrots and 2 peeled and cubed potatoes in the remaining oil, then add to the lentil mixture. Continue as above, replacing the figs with 100 g (3½ oz) chopped ready-to-eat dried apricots.

thai chickpea burgers

Serves **4**

Preparation time **20 minutes**

Cooking time **10 minutes**

4 spring onions

1 stalk **lemon grass**, outer
leaves removed

1.5 cm (¾ inch) piece of **fresh
ginger**, peeled and chopped

1 **red chilli**, halved and
deseeded

1 **garlic clove**, peeled

handful of **coriander leaves**

400 g (13 oz) can **chickpeas**,
drained

2 tablespoons **wholemeal
plain flour**

3 tablespoons **rapeseed oil**

salt and **pepper**

Pulse together the spring onions, lemon grass, ginger,
chilli, garlic and coriander leaves in a food processor
until finely chopped. Add the chickpeas and then pulse
again until roughly blended.

Add the flour and season with salt and pepper, then
process until the mixture forms a coarse thick paste.
Shape the mixture into 4 burgers.

Heat the oil in a frying pan, add the burgers and fry for
2–3 minutes on each side until browned. Serve with a
beansprout and pepper salad if liked.

For Mexican bean burgers, pulse together 4 spring
onions, 1 garlic clove, a handful of coriander leaves
and 1 teaspoon each chilli powder, ground cumin and
ground coriander in a food processor. Add a drained
400 g (13 oz) can mixed beans and pulse again until
roughly blended. Add 2 tablespoons wholemeal plain
flour and 3 tablespoons natural soya yogurt and season
with salt and pepper. Blend until the mixture forms a
coarse thick paste. Shape into 4 burgers and fry as
above. Serve in buns with guacamole and tomato salsa.

garlicky bean & mixed veg roast

Serves **4**
Preparation time **15 minutes**
Cooking time **40 minutes**

1 **green pepper**, cored,
   deseeded and cut into
   chunks
1 **red pepper**, cored,
   deseeded and cut into
   chunks
1 **yellow pepper**, cored,
   deseeded and cut into
   chunks
1 **aubergine**, trimmed and
   cut into chunks
1 **courgette**, trimmed and
   sliced
1 **red onion**, cut into wedges
a few **rosemary sprigs**
a few **thyme sprigs**
4 tablespoons **olive oil**
4 **tomatoes**, cut into wedges
125 g (4 oz) **closed cup
   mushrooms**, trimmed
4 **garlic cloves**, unpeeled
400 g (13 oz) can **flageolet
   beans**, drained
2 tablespoons **balsamic
   vinegar**
50 g (2 oz) **black olives**
salt and **pepper**

Put the peppers, aubergine, courgette, onion, rosemary and thyme in a large roasting tin. Drizzle over the oil, season with salt and pepper and toss until evenly coated in the oil, then spread out in a single layer. Roast a preheated oven, 200°C (400°F), Gas Mark 6, for 20 minutes until starting to soften.

Add the tomatoes, mushrooms and garlic cloves and mix with the other vegetables, then roast for a further 10 minutes until all the vegetables are tender.

Squeeze the soft garlic out of its skin on to the vegetables in the tin. Add the beans and vinegar and mix well. Return to the oven for a final 10 minutes. Scatter over the olives and serve with crusty bread.

For roasted vegetable tart, put 3 mixed-coloured peppers, cored, deseeded and cut into chunks, in a roasting tin with 1 onion, cut into wedges, and 1 sliced courgette. Drizzle with 3 tablespoons olive oil, season with salt and pepper and toss until evenly coated in the oil, then spread out in a single layer. Roast in a preheated, 200°C (400°F), Gas Mark 6, for 20 minutes until tender and lightly charred. Add 3 tomatoes, cut into wedges, scatter over 2 chopped garlic cloves and 1 tablespoon each chopped rosemary and thyme. Drizzle over 2 tablespoons balsamic vinegar and toss all the ingredients together. Unroll a 375 g (12 oz) sheet of ready-rolled vegan puff pastry on to a baking sheet. Spread the vegetables over the pastry, leaving a border around the edge, and bake in the oven for 20–25 minutes until the pastry is crisp and golden.

pak choi with chilli & ginger

Serves **4**

Preparation time **5 minutes**

Cooking time **5 minutes**

1 tablespoon **groundnut oil**

½ **chilli**, sliced into rings

1 tablespoon peeled and
chopped **fresh root ginger**

large pinch of **salt**

500 g (1 lb) **pak choi**, leaves
separated

100 ml (3½ fl oz) **water**

¼ teaspoon **sesame oil**

Heat the groundnut oil in a wok or large frying pan over a high heat until the oil starts to shimmer. Add the chilli, ginger and salt and stir-fry for 15 seconds.

Tip the pak choi into the pan and stir-fry for 1 minute, then add the measurement water and continue cooking and stirring until the pak choi is tender and the water has evaporated.

Add the sesame oil to the pan, toss well and serve immediately.

herby quinoa stuffed tomatoes

Serves **4**

Preparation time **20 minutes**

Cooking time **40–50 minutes**

50 g (2 oz) **quinoa**, rinsed and
drained

4 large **beef tomatoes**

½ small **red onion**, finely
chopped

75 g (3 oz) **roasted peppers**
from a jar, drained and sliced

1 **red chilli**, deseeded and
chopped

2 tablespoons chopped **flat
leaf parsley**

2 tablespoon chopped
coriander

2 tablespoons **sunflower
seeds**

1 teaspoon **sesame oil**

1 tablespoon **soy sauce**, plus
extra to serve

2 tablespoons **olive oil**

pepper

Add the quinoa to a saucepan of boiling water, then
simmer for 10–12 minutes until tender. Drain, rinse in
cold water and drain again.

Meanwhile, cut the tops off the tomatoes and hollow
out the centres with a teaspoon. Put half the tomato
pulp and seeds in a bowl, discarding the rest, add the
onion, peppers, chilli, parsley, coriander and sunflower
seeds and mix well.

Stir the sesame oil and soy sauce together and pour
into the bowl. Mix well, then add the quinoa and mix
again. Season with pepper; the soy sauce is salty, so
you won't need to add extra salt.

Sit the tomato shells on a baking sheet. Spoon the
quinoa mixture into the tomatoes, drizzle with the
olive oil and bake a preheated oven, 190°C (375°F),
Gas Mark 5, for 30–35 minutes until the tomatoes
are tender.

For slow-roasted tomato quinoa salad, cook the
quinoa, then rinse and drain as above. Cut 6 tomatoes
in half and put in a roasting tin with 1 thinly sliced garlic
clove and a few thyme and rosemary sprigs. Drizzle over
2 tablespoons olive oil, season with salt and pepper
and bake in a preheated oven, 160°C (325°F), Gas
Mark 3, for about 1 ½ hours until very soft. Mix the
tomatoes and their juices from the tin with the cooked
quinoa, 1 small red onion, thinly sliced, 1 finely chopped
red chilli and 2 tablespoons each sunflower seeds and
chopped flat leaf parsley. Mix 1 tablespoon soy sauce
and 1 teaspoon sesame oil together, pour over the salad
and toss to mix. Serve with rocket or watercress.

gnocchi in tomato & leek sauce

Serves 4
Preparation time **30 minutes**
Cooking time **25 minutes**

625 g (1¼ lb) **floury
 potatoes**, such as King
 Edward or Maris Piper,
 scrubbed
125 g (4 oz) **plain flour**
salt and **pepper**

Sauce
1 tablespoon **olive oil**
1 **leek**, trimmed, cleaned and
 chopped
1 **garlic clove**, crushed
4 **ripe tomatoes**, roughly
 chopped
1 tablespoon **tomato purée**
pinch of **sugar**
small handful of torn **basil
 leaves**
salt and **pepper**

Cook the potatoes in their skins in a large saucepan of salted boiling water for about 20 minutes, until tender. Drain and leave until cool enough to handle but not cold.

Meanwhile, make the sauce. Heat the oil in a frying pan, add the leek and cook over a medium heat for 5 minutes until tender. Add the garlic and tomatoes and cook for 5 minutes until the tomatoes are soft. Stir in the tomato purée and a little water to make a sauce. Add the sugar, season with salt and pepper and simmer for 3 minutes.

Peel off the potato skins and pass the potatoes through a potato ricer or mash with a potato masher until smooth. Season with salt and pepper, then knead in the flour to form a dough. Divide the gnocchi dough into 4 pieces and roll each piece into a thick sausage. Cut into 1.5 cm (¾ inch) pieces and press with the prongs of a fork to mark a ridged pattern.

Cook the gnocchi in a large saucepan of salted boiling water for 1–2 minutes until they float to the surface. Remove from the pan with a slotted spoon and add to the sauce. Add the basil and gently turn the gnocchi to coat in the sauce. Serve with an extra grinding of pepper.

For fried gnocchi with broccoli & lemon, make the gnocchi as above (or use shop-bought vegan gnocchi). Cook 300 g (10 oz) broccoli, cut into florets, in a saucepan of boiling salted water for 3 minutes until just tender, then drain. Meanwhile, heat 3 tablespoons olive oil in a large frying pan, add the gnocchi and fry for 8–10 minutes until golden and crisp. Stir in 1 chopped red chilli, 1 crushed garlic clove, finely grated rind of 1 lemon and the broccoli and heat through for 3 minutes.

roasted stuffed peppers

Serves **2**

Preparation time **10 minutes**

Cooking time **1 hour**

4 large **red peppers**

2 **garlic cloves**, crushed

1 tablespoon **chopped thyme**,
   plus extra to garnish

4 **plum tomatoes**, halved

4 tablespoons **extra virgin
   olive oil**

2 tablespoons **balsamic
   vinegar**

salt and **pepper**

Cut the red peppers in half lengthways, then scoop out and discard the cores and seeds. Put the pepper halves, cut-side up, in a roasting tin lined with foil or a ceramic dish. Divide the garlic and thyme between them and season with salt and pepper.

Put a tomato half in each pepper and drizzle with the oil and vinegar. Roast in a preheated oven, 220°C (425°F), Gas Mark 7, for 55 minutes–1 hour until the peppers are soft and charred.

Serve with some crusty bread to mop up the juices and a baby leaf salad if liked.

For roasted stuffed mushrooms, place 4 large portobello mushrooms, trimmed, gill-side up on a baking sheet and lightly brush with 1 tablespoon olive oil. Roast in a preheated oven, 220°C (425°F), Gas Mark 7, for 10 minutes. Meanwhile, roughly chop 1 large plum tomato and toss in a small bowl with 1 thinly sliced garlic clove, 1 tablespoon chopped thyme leaves, 1 teaspoon balsamic vinegar and plenty of salt and pepper. Remove from the oven and spoon the tomato filling into the mushrooms, slightly piling it around the stems. Return to the oven for a further 10 minutes until the filling is softened. Serve on warmed serving plates with the juices spooned alongside together with warm crusty bread to mop up the juices.

cauliflower & butternut balti

Serves **4**

Preparation time **15 minutes**

Cooking time **20 minutes**

1 tablespoon **sunflower oil**

1 **onion**, chopped

1 **red pepper**, cored, deseeded and cut into chunks

1 teaspoon **mustard seeds**

1 teaspoon **fennel seeds**

2 **garlic cloves**, crushed

1.5 cm (¾ inch) piece of **fresh root ginger**, peeled and grated

2 teaspoons **garam masala**

2 teaspoons **ground cumin**

1 teaspoon **ground coriander**

1 teaspoon **ground turmeric**

½ teaspoon **dried chilli flakes**

450 g (14½ oz) **butternut squash**, peeled, deseeded and cut into chunks

1 **cauliflower**, cut into florets

400 g (13 oz) can **chopped tomatoes**

300 ml (½ pint) **water**

200 g (7 oz) **frozen peas**

125 g (4 oz) **cashew nuts**, toasted

salt and pepper

Heat the oil in a large saucepan, add the onion and red pepper and cook over a medium heat for 3 minutes until softened. Add the mustard and fennel seeds and cook for 30 seconds until starting to pop and smell fragrant. Add the garlic, ginger, garam masala, cumin, coriander, turmeric and chilli flakes and cook, stirring, for 30 seconds.

Add the butternut squash and cauliflower and stir to coat in the spices. Stir in the tomatoes and measurement water, season with salt and pepper and bring to the boil, then cover and simmer for 10 minutes, stirring occasionally, until the vegetables are tender. Add the peas and cook for a further 3 minutes.

Stir in half the cashew nuts and sprinkle the rest on the top to garnish. Serve with naan bread.

For cauliflower, coconut & spinach balti, heat 3 tablespoons sunflower oil in a large saucepan, add 1 chopped onion and 1 chopped red chilli and cook over a medium heat for 3 minutes until softened. Add 3 tablespoons vegan balti curry paste and cook, stirring, for 30 seconds. Add 1 cauliflower, cut into florets, and 250 g (8 oz) new potatoes, scrubbed, and turn to coat in the spices. Stir in a 400 g (13 oz) can chopped tomatoes and 200 ml (7 fl oz) coconut milk, season with salt and pepper and bring to the boil, then cover and simmer for 10 minutes until the cauliflower and potatoes are just cooked. Add 200 g (7 oz) frozen peas and cook for 3 minutes, then stir in 250 g (8 oz) spinach leaves until just wilted. Sprinkle with toasted flaked almonds to serve.

nut roast parcels

Serves **4**
Preparation time **30 minutes**
Cooking time **30 minutes**

3 tablespoons **rapeseed oil**
1 **onion**, finely chopped
½ **red pepper**, cored,
    deseeded and finely
    chopped
1 **celery stick**, finely chopped
1 **carrot**, peeled and coarsely
    grated
75 g (3 oz) **chestnut
    mushrooms**, trimmed and
    finely chopped
1 teaspoon **yeast extract**
50 g (2 oz) **fresh white
    breadcrumbs**
75 g (3 oz) **mixed nuts**,
    such as pistachio, blanched
    almonds and cooked
    chestnuts, finely chopped
2 tablespoons **pine nuts**
2 tablespoons chopped
    flat leaf parsley
1 tablespoon chopped
    rosemary
1 tablespoon **wholemeal
    plain flour**
8 sheets of **filo pastry**
green beans and roasted
    cherry tomatoes, to serve

Heat 1 tablespoon of the oil in a frying pan, add the onion, red pepper and celery and cook over a gentle heat for 5 minutes until softened. Add the carrot and mushrooms and cook for a further 5 minutes until all the vegetables are tender.

Remove the pan from the heat and stir in the yeast extract, breadcrumbs, nuts, pine nuts, parsley, rosemary and flour. Season with salt and pepper and mix together.

Brush one sheet of filo pastry with some of the remaining oil, then place a second on top. Spoon one-quarter of the nut mixture on to one end of the filo pastry and roll up, tucking in the ends as you roll to encase the filling. Put on a baking sheet. Repeat with the remaining pastry and filling to make 4 rolls. Brush the tops with oil.

Bake the parcels in a preheated oven, 190°C (375°F), Gas Mark 5, for 20 minutes until golden and crisp. Serve with green beans and roasted cherry tomatoes.

For nut roast meatballs, heat 1 tablespoon oil in a frying pan, add 1 finely chopped onion, 1 finely chopped celery stick and 1 crushed garlic clove and cook over a gentle heat for 5 minutes until softened. Add 1 peeled and coarsely grated carrot, ½ coarsely grated courgette and 125 g (4 oz) mushrooms, finely chopped, and cook for 5 minutes until tender. Remove from the heat and stir in the yeast extract, breadcrumbs, mixed nuts (omitting the pine nuts), herbs, flour and salt and pepper as above. Roll into 20 small balls, place on a baking sheet and bake in a preheated oven, 200°C (400°F), Gas Mark 6, for 15 minutes until golden. Serve with spaghetti tossed in a jar of vegan tomato pasta sauce.

mixed vegetable chop suey

Serves **4**

Preparation time **10 minutes**

Cooking time **8 minutes**

1 tablespoon **cornflour**

1 tablespoon **light soy sauce**

1 tablespoon **rice wine** or
   dry sherry

3 tablespoons **vegetable
   stock** or **water**

½ teaspoon **agave syrup**

2 tablespoons **groundnut oil**

2 **red peppers**, cored,
   deseeded and cut into strips

2 **shallots**, finely sliced

1 teaspoon peeled and
   chopped **fresh root ginger**

2 **garlic cloves**, chopped

150 g (5 oz) **shiitake
   mushrooms**, trimmed
   and halved

50 g (2 oz) canned **sliced
   bamboo shoots**, drained

50 g (2 oz) drained canned
   water chestnuts

300 g (10 oz) **bean sprouts**

3 **spring onions**, cut into
   2.5 cm (1 inch) lengths

Put the cornflour in a jug with the soy sauce and rice
wine or sherry and mix to a smooth paste. Stir in the
stock or measurement water and agave syrup and set
the sauce aside.

Heat the oil in a wok or large frying pan over a high
heat until the oil starts to shimmer. Add the red peppers,
shallots, ginger and garlic and stir-fry for 2 minutes,
then add the mushrooms, bamboo shoots and water
chestnuts and stir-fry for a further 2 minutes.

Add the bean sprouts to the pan with the spring onions
and the prepared sauce. Continue cooking for 1–2
minutes, or until the vegetables are coated in a rich
velvety glaze. Serve immediately.

For pepper & mushroom chop suey-style noodles,
make the sauce as above and set aside. Heat the
oil in a wok or large frying pan as above, add 1 red
pepper, cored, deseeded and cut into strips, 250 g
(8 oz) chestnut mushrooms, trimmed and quartered,
and 2 finely sliced shallots and stir-fry for 3–4 minutes
until softened and golden. Add 1 teaspoon peeled
and chopped fresh root ginger and 6 finely chopped
spring onions and stir-fry for 1 minute. Meanwhile,
cook 175 g (6 oz) dried rice noodles according to the
packet instructions, then drain and set aside. Add the
noodles to the pan along with the sauce and gently toss
together for 2 minutes until piping hot. Serve in deep
warmed serving bowls with chopsticks.

basil & pine nut risotto

Serves **4**
Preparation time **20 minutes**
Cooking time **25 minutes**

200 g (7 oz) **baby plum tomatoes**
3 tablespoons **olive oil**
2 **red onions**, thinly sliced
1 **garlic clove**, thinly sliced
4 tablespoons **pine nuts**
200 g (7 oz) **Arborio rice**
150 ml (¼ pint) **white wine**
about 600 ml (1 pint) **vegetable stock**, plus extra if needed
6 tablespoons chopped **basil leaves**
salt and **pepper**
vegan hard Parmesan-style cheese, finely grated, to serve

Put the tomatoes in a roasting tin and toss with 1 tablespoon of the oil until evenly coated, then spread out in a single layer. Roast in a preheated oven, 200°C (400°F), Gas Mark 6, for 20 minutes until soft and lightly charred in places.

Meanwhile, heat the remaining oil in a large, heavy-based frying pan, add the onions and garlic and cook over a medium-high heat for 5 minutes until softened and beginning to turn golden.

Toast the pine nuts in a dry frying pan over a medium heat, shaking the pan occasionally, for 2–3 minutes until golden. Set aside.

Add the rice to the onions and garlic and stir well to coat. Pour in the wine and half the stock and bring to the boil, then simmer gently, stirring, until the liquid is almost all absorbed. Stir in the remaining stock, then simmer gently, stirring frequently, for a further 10–12 minutes until it is almost all absorbed and the rice is tender and cooked through, adding more stock if necessary. Add the basil and cook for 2–3 minutes until wilted, then mix in the pine nuts.

Stir half the roasted tomatoes through the risotto and season well with salt and pepper. Serve in warmed serving bowls topped with the remaining tomatoes.

caper, lemon & chilli spaghetti

Serves **4**

Preparation time **5 minutes**

Cooking time **12 minutes**

350 g (11½ oz) **spelt spaghetti**

200 g (7 oz) **Tenderstem broccoli,** cut into chunks

2 tablespoons **olive oil**

1 small **red onion**, finely sliced

1 **red chilli**, deseeded and chopped

2 tablespoons **capers**

finely grated rind of 1 **lemon** and 1 tablespoon juice

2 tablespoons **balsamic vinegar**

salt and **pepper**

Cook the spaghetti in a large saucepan of salted boiling water for 10 minutes, adding the broccoli for the final 3 minutes, or until just tender.

Meanwhile, heat the oil in a frying pan, add the onion and chilli and cook over a gentle heat for 2 minutes. Stir in the capers, lemon rind and juice and vinegar, season with salt and pepper and heat through.

Drain the spaghetti and broccoli, reserving 1 tablespoon of the cooking water and adding to the caper mixture. Add the drained spaghetti and broccoli to the pan and toss well to combine over the heat. Serve with an extra grinding of pepper.

For artichoke, lemon & mint spaghetti, cook 350 g (11½ oz) of spaghetti as above, adding 125 g (4 oz) frozen peas for the final 3 minutes until just tender. Meanwhile, heat 2 tablespoons olive oil in a frying pan, add a drained 290 g (9¾ oz) jar marinated artichokes in oil and heat through for 1 minute. Stir in the finely grated rind of 1 lemon, 1 tablespoon lemon juice and 2 tablespoons each balsamic vinegar and chopped mint and season with salt and pepper. Drain the spaghetti and peas, reserving 1 tablespoon of the cooking water and adding to the artichoke mixture. Add the drained spaghetti and peas to the pan and toss well to combine over the heat. Serve with an extra grinding of pepper.

veggie kebabs with bulgar wheat

Serves **4**
Preparation time **20 minutes**
Cooking time **20–25 minutes**

1 small **red pepper**, cored,
   deseeded and cut into chunks
1 small **yellow pepper**, cored,
   deseeded and cut into chunks
2 small **courgettes**, trimmed
   and thickly sliced
1 small **aubergine**, trimmed
   and cut into chunks
1 small **red onion**, quartered
8 **chestnut mushrooms**,
   trimmed and halved
2 teaspoons **dried rosemary**
1 teaspoon **fennel seeds**
finely grated rind of 1 **lemon**
2 tablespoons **olive oil**
salt and **pepper**

Bulgar wheat salad
750 ml (1 ¼ pint) **vegetable
   stock**
250 g (8 oz) **coarse bulgar
   wheat**
1 tablespoon **harissa**
75 g (3 oz) **raisins**
2 **spring onions**, finely sliced
2 tablespoons chopped **mint**
50 g (2 oz) **sunflower seeds**

Put the vegetables in a bowl with the rosemary, fennel seeds and lemon rind. Drizzle over the oil, season and toss until the vegetables are evenly coated in the oil.

Thread the different vegetables alternately on to 4 long or 8 short metal skewers and cook under a preheated medium-hot grill for 20–25 minutes, or until tender and browned, turning occasionally.

Meanwhile, bring the stock to the boil in a saucepan. Add the bulgar wheat, cover and simmer for 7 minutes. Remove from the heat and leave to stand until the stock is absorbed.

Fork the harissa, raisins, spring onions, mint and sunflower seeds through the cooked bulgar wheat until combined, then spoon on to serving plates. Arrange the vegetable kebabs on the plates and serve immediately.

For roasted vegetables with harissa bulgar wheat, put 1 small red and 1 small yellow pepper, cored and cut into chunks, in a roasting tin with 2 small courgettes, thickly sliced, and 1 red onion, cut into wedges. Sprinkle over 2 tablespoons olive oil, 1 tablespoon chopped rosemary leaves and 1 teaspoon fennel seeds and toss. Roast a preheated oven, 200°C (400°F), Gas Mark 6, for 25 minutes until softened and charred in places. Meanwhile, add 250 g (8 oz) bulgar wheat to 750 ml (1 ¼ pints) vegetable stock in a saucepan and bring to the boil, then simmer gently, stirring, for 7 minutes. Remove from the heat and leave to stand until the stock is absorbed. Add 1 tablespoon harissa and 2 tablespoons chopped mint, season with salt and pepper and fork together, then stir in the roasted vegetables.

potato, rosemary & onion pie

Serves **4**

Preparation time **30 minutes**

Cooking time **about 45 minutes**

8 tablespoons **olive oil**

1 large **Spanish onion**, halved and thinly sliced

1 kg (2 lb) **potatoes**, scrubbed and thinly sliced

5 tablespoons chopped **rosemary leaves**

½ teaspoon **dried chilli flakes**

½ teaspoon **ground cumin**

½ teaspoon **ground coriander**

150 ml (¼ pint) **vegetable stock**

500 g (1 lb) **ready-made vegan puff pastry**

plain flour, for dusting

2 tablespoons **soya milk**

salt and **pepper**

Heat half the oil in a frying pan, add the onion and cook over a medium-high heat for 5 minutes until softened and beginning to turn golden. Remove and set aside. Heat the remaining oil in the pan, add the potato slices, rosemary and spices and cook, tossing and stirring frequently, for 10 minutes until softened and lightly golden.

Layer the potato slices in a large pie dish with the onions. Pour over the stock and season with salt and pepper.

Roll the pastry out on a lightly floured surface to about 1.5 cm (¾ inch) wider than the top of the pie dish. Cut a thin strip of pastry and place around the edge of the dish, pressing down with a little water to seal. Lightly brush the top of the strip with water, top with the pastry lid and press around the edges with a fork to seal. Make an incision in the centre of the pie for the steam to escape and lightly brush all over with the soya milk.

Bake in a preheated oven, 220°C (425°F), Gas Mark 7, for 25–30 minutes until the pastry is golden and the potatoes are tender. Serve hot.

For sweet potato & red onion pie with thyme, heat 4 tablespoons olive oil in a frying pan, add 2 thinly sliced red onions and cook over a medium-high heat for 5 minutes until softened. Remove and set aside. Heat another 4 tablespoons olive oil in the pan, add 1 kg (2 lb) sweet potatoes, peeled and thinly sliced, and cook over a medium heat, tossing and stirring frequently, for 10 minutes. Add 1 tablespoon ground coriander and ½ teaspoon dried chilli flakes and cook for a further minute. Follow the recipe above to layer in a pie dish with the onions, add the stock, top the pie with pastry and bake.

pea & mint pesto fettuccine

Serves **4**
Preparation time **20 minutes**
Cooking time **10–12 minutes**

250 g (8 oz) **dried egg-free
   fettuccine**
250 g (8 oz) **frozen peas**,
   thawed
1 **garlic clove**, roughly
   chopped
1 teaspoon **wasabi**
5 tablespoons **mint leaves**
6 tablespoons **olive oil**
2 tablespoons **pine nuts**
150 ml (¼ pint) **water**
salt and **pepper**
mint leaves, to garnish
crusty bread, to serve

Cook the fettuccine in a large saucepan of lightly salted boiling water for 8–10 minutes until just tender.

Meanwhile, blend together the peas, garlic, wasabi, mint, oil, pine nuts and measurement water in a blender or food processor until well combined. Season with plenty of salt and pepper.

Drain the pasta well and return to the pan with the pea pesto. Toss over a gentle heat for 2–3 minutes until piping hot. Sprinkle with the mint leaves and serve immediately in warmed serving bowls with crusty bread.

For basil pesto with fettuccine, cook 350 g (1 1½ oz) dried egg-free fettuccine as above. Meanwhile, blend together 1 whole garlic clove, 2 handfuls of basil leaves, 6 tablespoons olive oil and 3 tablespoons pine nuts in a blender or food processor until smooth. Season well with salt and pepper. Drain the pasta well and return to the pan with the basil pesto. Toss over a gentle heat for 1–2 minutes until piping hot, then serve immediately in warmed serving bowls.

sage & tomato pilaff

Preparation time **15 minutes**
Cooking time **40–45 minutes**
Serves **4**

500 g (1 lb) **plum tomatoes**
1 **red pepper**, cored,
   deseeded and quartered
1 **onion**, roughly chopped
2 tablespoons **olive oil**
small bunch of **sage**
200 g (7 oz) **mixed easy-
   cook white long-grain** and
   wild rice
salt and **pepper**

Cut each tomato into 8 and thickly slice the pepper quarters. Place in a roasting tin with the onion, then drizzle with the oil and season well with salt and pepper. Tear some of the sage into pieces and sprinkle over the vegetables. Roast in a preheated oven, 200°C (400°F), Gas Mark 6, for 40–45 minutes until the vegetables are softened.

Meanwhile, cook the rice in a saucepan of boiling water for 15 minutes, or until only just cooked.

Drain the cooked rice and mix into the roasted vegetables. Spoon into warmed serving bowls and sprinkle with the remaining sage leaves. Serve with warm ciabatta or herb bread.

For sage & tomato Camargue rice with olives, heat 3 tablespoons olive oil in a large, heavy-based frying pan, add 1 large onion, finely chopped, and 1 red pepper, cored, deseeded and roughly chopped, and cook over a medium-high heat for 3–4 minutes until softened. Stir in 5 tablespoons roughly chopped sage and 300 g (10 oz) Camargue red rice, then add 600 ml (1 pint) vegetable stock. Bring to the boil, then cover and simmer very gently, stirring occasionally, for 20 minutes, or until the rice is tender and cooked through, adding a little more stock if necessary. Meanwhile, heat 1 tablespoon olive oil in a separate frying pan, add 250 g (8 oz) cherry tomatoes and cook gently for 3–4 minutes until softened and the skins have burst. Stir into the rice once the rice is cooked, season with salt and pepper and serve.

cauliflower & chickpea pan-fry

Serves **4**

Preparation time **20 minutes**

Cooking time **20 minutes**

6 tablespoons **olive oil**

1 **red onion**, cut into thin wedges

½ **cauliflower**, cut into small florets

1 teaspoon **garam masala**

1 teaspoon **ground coriander**

4 tablespoons **water**, plus 150 ml (¼ pint)

28 **chard leaves**, washed, patted dry and cut into strips

1 teaspoon **cumin seeds**

1 **garlic clove**, thinly sliced

400 g (13 oz) can **chickpeas**, drained and rinsed

5 tablespoons **tahini**

4 tablespoons **lemon juice**

salt and **pepper**

naan bread, to serve

Heat the oil in a large, heavy-based frying pan or wok, add the onion and cook over a medium-high heat, stirring frequently, for 3–4 minutes until beginning to soften. Add the cauliflower florets, the garam masala and the ground coriander and cook for 5 minutes, stirring almost constantly to prevent the cauliflower from catching, then add the 4 tablespoons cold water and cook for a further 2 minutes, stirring almost constantly.

Stir the chard leaves, cumin seeds and garlic into the pan and cook, stirring, for a further 2 minutes. Add the chickpeas along with the tahini, lemon juice and 150 ml (¼ pint) measurement water and season with salt and pepper. Toss the vegetables in the sauce, then reduce the heat, cover and simmer for 2 minutes. Season generously with salt and pepper.

Toss again before serving in warmed serving bowls with naan bread.

For curried broccoli pan-fry with cumin seeds,

heat 3 tablespoons olive oil in a large, heavy-based frying pan or wok, add 1 large white onion, thinly sliced into wedges, and stir-fry over a medium-high heat for 2 minutes. Add 300 g (10 oz) small broccoli florets and 1 red pepper, cored, deseeded and thinly sliced, and stir-fry for 3–4 minutes until softened. Add 2 tablespoons curry paste and 1 teaspoon cumin seeds and cook, stirring, for a further 1 minute. Add 2 tablespoons mango chutney, season with salt and pepper if necessary and toss again for 1 minute. Serve piled on to 2 warmed, halved naan breads.

ratatouille pie with parsnip mash

Serves **6**
Preparation time **25 minutes**
Cooking time **45 minutes**

5 tablespoons **olive oil**
1 **red pepper**, cored,
    deseeded and cut into
    chunks
1 **green pepper**, cored,
    deseeded and cut into
    chunks
1 **yellow pepper**, cored,
    deseeded and cut into
    chunks
1 **garlic clove**, thinly sliced
1 large **aubergine**, trimmed
    and cut into chunks
2 **courgettes**, trimmed and cut
    into chunks
5 **tomatoes**, roughly chopped
150 ml (¼ pint) **red wine**
150 ml (¼ pint) **water**
1 **vegetable stock cube**
1.125 kg (2½ lb) **parsnips**,
    peeled and chopped
2 tablespoons **soya spread**
1 tablespoon chopped **thyme
    leaves**
salt and **pepper**

Heat the oil in a large, heavy-based frying pan, add the peppers, garlic, aubergine and courgettes and cook over a medium-high heat, stirring and tossing occasionally, for 10 minutes until softened and lightly golden in places. Add the tomatoes and cook for 3 minutes. Pour in the wine and measurement water and bring to the boil, then cover and simmer for a further 10 minutes.

Meanwhile, bring a large saucepan of lightly salted water to the boil, crumble in the stock cube with the parsnips and mix well. Bring to a gentle simmer and cook for 10 minutes until the parsnips are tender. Drain well, return to the pan and mash with the soya spread, then stir in the thyme leaves.

Transfer the ratatouille mixture to a large gratin dish. Spoon the mashed parsnips over the vegetables and season generously with pepper. Bake in a preheated oven, 200°C (400°F), Gas Mark 6, for 20 minutes until the top is lightly golden in places. Serve with a simple green salad.

For roasted vegetable & parsnip tray bake, cut 3 different-coloured peppers into chunks, then put in a large roasting tin along with 2 courgettes, trimmed and cut into chunks, and 2 parsnips, peeled and cut into chunks. Drizzle with 4 tablespoons olive oil, sprinkle with 2 tablespoons chopped rosemary and season with salt and pepper. Roast in a preheated oven, 200°C (400°F), Gas Mark 6, for 20 minutes until soft and lightly golden in places. Add 4 tomatoes, cut into chunks, to the tin and gently toss, then roast for a further 10 minutes. Serve hot in warmed serving bowls with crusty bread to mop up the juices.

squash, carrot & mango tagine

Serves **4**

Preparation time **15 minutes**

Cooking time **35–40 minutes**

2 tablespoons **olive oil**

1 large **onion**, cut into large chunks

3 **garlic cloves**, finely chopped

1 **butternut squash**, about 875 g (1¾ lb), peeled, deseeded and cubed

2 small **carrots**, peeled and cut into thick batons

½ x 2.5 cm (1 inch) **cinnamon stick**

½ teaspoon **ground turmeric**

¼ teaspoon **cayenne pepper** (optional)

½ teaspoon **ground cumin**

1 teaspoon **paprika**

pinch of **saffron threads**

1 tablespoon **tomato purée**

750 ml (1¼ pints) **hot vegetable stock**

1 **mango**, peeled, stoned and cut into 2.5 cm (1 inch) chunks

salt and **pepper**

2 tablespoons chopped **coriander**, to garnish

Heat the oil in a large, heavy-based saucepan, add the onion and cook over a gentle heat for 5 minutes until beginning to soften. Add the garlic, butternut squash, carrots and spices and cook gently for 5 minutes.

Stir in the tomato purée, then pour in the stock and season with salt and pepper. Cover and simmer gently for 20–25 minutes until the vegetables are tender. Stir in the mango and simmer gently for a further 5 minutes.

Ladle the tagine into serving bowls, sprinkle with the coriander to garnish and serve with steamed couscous.

For spicy squash & carrot soup, make the tagine as above, adding an extra 250 ml (8 fl oz) hot vegetable stock. Once the vegetables are tender, transfer to a blender or food processor and blend until smooth. Ladle into bowls and serve scattered with chopped coriander and topped with a swirl of natural vegan yogurt.

aubergine & wheatberries salad

Serves **4**

Preparation time **20 minutes**,
   plus standing and cooling

Cooking time about **5 minutes**

8 tablespoons **olive oil**
225 g (7½ oz) **wheatberries**
1 teaspoon **ground coriander**
½ teaspoon **ground paprika**
½ teaspoon **chilli powder**
450 ml (¾ pint) **vegetable
   stock**
1 large **aubergine**, trimmed
   and cut into 1.5 cm (¾ inch)
   cubes
100 g (4 oz) **walnut pieces**
finely grated rind of 1 **lemon**
50 g (2 oz) fresh **baby
   spinach leaves**
handful of **coriander leaves**
salt and **pepper**
lemon wedges, to serve

Heat 1 tablespoon of the oil in a large, heavy-based
saucepan, add the wheatberries and spices and toss
well to coat. Pour in the stock and bring to the boil,
stirring constantly. Cover with a tight-fitting lid, remove
from the heat and leave to stand for 25 minutes until all
the liquid is absorbed and the grain is tender.

Meanwhile, heat the remaining oil in a heavy-based
frying pan, add the aubergine cubes and cook over a
medium-high heat, turning occasionally, for 4–5 minutes
until golden all over and tender. Add the walnuts and
toss over the heat for 1 minute.

Transfer the wheatberries to a large bowl and toss with
the lemon rind, aubergine and walnuts, then leave to
cool for a few minutes before adding the spinach and
coriander leaves. Toss well and season with a little salt
and plenty of pepper, then serve with lemon wedges.

For courgette & onion salad with barley couscous
& coriander, heat 1 tablespoon olive oil in a saucepan,
add 225 g (7½ oz) barley couscous and ½ teaspoon
each ground paprika and chilli powder and toss well
to coat. Pour in 450 ml (¾ pint) vegetable stock and
bring to the boil, stirring constantly. Cover with a tight-
fitting lid, remove from the heat and leave to stand for
20 minutes. Meanwhile, heat 4 tablespoons olive oil
in a large, heavy-based frying pan, add 2 courgettes,
trimmed and cubed, and cook over a medium-heat,
turning occasionally, for 4–5 minutes until golden all
over and tender. Toss into the swollen couscous along
with 2 handfuls of coriander leaves, finely grated rind
of 1 lemon and a little salt and plenty of pepper. Serve
with lemon wedges.

pearl barley risotto with carrots

Serves **4**
Preparation time **15 minutes**, plus standing
Cooking time **25 minutes**

225 g (7½ oz) **pearl barley**
400 g (14 oz) **baby carrots**, scrubbed
5 tablespoons **olive oil**
1 large **onion**, finely chopped
1 large **leek**, trimmed, cleaned and thinly sliced
1 **garlic clove**, thinly sliced
1 tablespoon **thyme leaves**
1 teaspoon **ground coriander**
1.2 litres (2 pints) **vegetable stock**, plus extra if needed
2 tablespoons chopped **flat leaf parsley**, to garnish
salt and **pepper**
wholemeal bread, to serve

Put the pearl barley in a bowl, pour over enough boiling water to cover and leave to stand for 10 minutes.

Toss the carrots in a shallow roasting tin with 2 tablespoons of the oil until evenly coated, then roast in a preheated oven, 200°C (400°F), Gas Mark 6, for 20 minutes until tender and lightly charred in places.

Meanwhile, heat the remaining oil in a frying pan, add the onion and leek with the garlic and thyme and cook over a medium heat, stirring occasionally, for 4 minutes until soft and pale golden. Stir in the ground coriander and cook for a further 1 minute.

Drain the pearl barley, add to the frying pan with half the stock and bring to the boil. Cover and simmer very gently, stirring occasionally, for about 10 minutes until almost all the stock is absorbed. Add the remaining stock and stir, then cover and simmer gently again until the pearl barley is tender and some of the stock is still left in the pan, adding more stock if necessary.

Add the roasted carrots to the risotto and stir through. Season and serve with warm wholemeal bread.

For roasted root vegetable risotto, put 200 g (7 oz) scrubbed baby carrots into a roasting tin with 2 parsnips, peeled and cut into batons, and 225 g (7½ oz) peeled and chopped turnips. Add 3 tablespoons olive oil and toss. Add 1 tablespoon chopped rosemary leaves and toss again. Roast in a preheated oven, 200°C (400°F), Gas Mark 6, for 20–25 minutes until lightly charred and tender. Meanwhile, cook the onion, leek and garlic as above, omitting the thyme, then add and cook the pearl barley as above. Fold in the roasted veg and season.

roasted peppers with quinoa

Serves **4**

Preparation time **15 minutes**, plus standing

Cooking time **45 minutes**

2 **Romano** or **long red peppers**, halved, cored and deseeded

20 **yellow cherry tomatoes**, halved

2 large **yellow peppers**, halved, cored and deseeded

20 **red cherry tomatoes**, halved

1 teaspoon **cumin seeds**

2 tablespoons **olive oil**

200 g (7 oz) **quinoa**

1 **onion**, finely chopped

½ teaspoon **ground ginger**

1 teaspoon **paprika**

pinch of freshly grated **nutmeg**

50 g (2 oz) **ready-to-eat dried apricots**, chopped

50 g (2 oz) **raisins**

50 g (2 oz) **pitted dried dates**, chopped

50 g (2 oz) shelled **pistachio nuts**

25 g (1 oz) **flaked almonds**, toasted, plus extra to garnish

2 **spring onions**, finely sliced

salt and **pepper**

Fill the red peppers with the yellow tomatoes and the yellow peppers with the red tomatoes. Put in a roasting tin, scatter over the cumin seeds and drizzle with 1 tablespoon of the oil, then season well with salt and pepper. Roast in a preheated oven, 180°C (350°F), Gas Mark 4, for about 45 minutes, or until tender and slightly blackened around the edges.

Meanwhile, rinse the quinoa several times in cold water. Drain, put into a saucepan and cover with twice its volume of boiling water. Cover with a lid and simmer for about 12 minutes, or until the seed is coming away from the germ. Remove from the heat and leave to stand, covered, until all the water is absorbed.

Heat the remaining oil in a small frying pan, add the onion and cook over a gentle heat for 10 minutes until soft. Stir in the spices, dried fruits and nuts and cook, stirring frequently, for a further 3–4 minutes, or until the fruits have softened. Gently fold into the quinoa.

Heap the quinoa on to 4 plates and top each with 1 roasted red and 1 roasted yellow pepper half. Sprinkle with the spring onions and extra flaked almonds and serve.

vegetable paella with almonds

Serves **4**
Preparation time **25 minutes**
Cooking time **30 minutes**

4 tablespoons **olive oil**
1 **onion**, chopped
pinch of **saffron threads**
225 g (7½ oz) **Arborio rice**
1.2 litres (2 pints) **vegetable stock**
175 g (6 oz) fine **asparagus spears**, trimmed and cut into 5 cm (2 inch) lengths
bunch of **spring onions**, cut into strips
175 g (6 oz) **midi plum tomatoes** on the vine, halved
125 g (4 oz) **frozen peas**
3 tablespoons **flaked almonds**, toasted
3 tablespoons chopped **flat leaf parsley**
salt

Heat 1 tablespoon of the oil in a large, heavy-based frying pan, add the onion and saffron and cook over a medium heat, stirring frequently, for 5 minutes, until the onion is softened and golden. Add the rice and stir well, then season with some salt. Add the stock and bring to the boil, then cover and simmer, stirring occasionally, for 20 minutes until the stock is almost all absorbed and the rice is tender and cooked through.

Meanwhile, heat the remaining oil in a separate frying pan, add the asparagus and spring onions and cook over a medium heat for 5 minutes until softened and lightly charred in places. Remove from the pan with a slotted spoon. Add the vine tomatoes to the pan and cook for 2–3 minutes on each side until softened.

Add the peas to the rice and cook for a further 2 minutes, then add the asparagus, spring onions and tomatoes and gently toss through. Scatter with the almonds and parsley and serve.

For pepper & mushroom paella with pine nuts,

heat 2 tablespoons olive oil in a large, heavy-based frying pan, add 1 red, 1 green and 1 yellow pepper, cored, deseeded and thinly sliced, 175 g (6 oz) chestnut mushrooms, quartered, and 1 small red onion, thinly sliced, and cook over a medium heat for 4–5 minutes until softened. Add 225 g (7½ oz) Arborio rice and stir well, then season with some salt. Pour in 1.2 litres (2 pints) vegetable stock and bring to the boil, then cover and simmer for 20 minutes until the stock is almost all absorbed and the rice is tender and cooked through. Remove from the heat and stir in 3 tablespoons each lightly toasted pine nuts and chopped flat leaf parsley.

mushroom stroganoff

Serves **4**
Preparation time **15 minutes**
Cooking time **10 minutes**

5 tablespoons **olive oil**
450 g (14½ oz) **mixed
    mushrooms,** such as
    chestnut, chanterelle, shiitake
    and button, trimmed and
    halved or quartered if large
1 **garlic clove**, thinly sliced
1 large **red onion**, halved and
    thinly sliced
2 tablespoons **brandy**
1 teaspoon **wholegrain
    mustard**
½ teaspoon **English mustard**
½ teaspoon **ground paprika**
2 tablespoons **cashew butter**
250 ml (9 fl oz) **soya cream**
4 tablespoons chopped **flat
    leaf parsley**
salt and **pepper**

Heat the oil in a large, heavy-based frying pan, add
the mushrooms, garlic and onion and cook over a high
heat, stirring occasionally, for 5 minutes until golden and
softened.

Add the brandy, mustards and paprika and continue to
cook, stirring and tossing constantly, for 1–2 minutes.
Stir in the cashew butter and soya cream and gently
heat for 1 minute until piping hot but not boiling,
otherwise the cream may separate.

Stir in the chopped parsley and season with a little salt
and plenty of pepper. Serve on a bed of rice.

For vegetable stroganoff, heat 3 tablespoons olive oil
in a large, heavy-based frying pan, add 1 large onion,
thinly sliced, 2 sweet potatoes, peeled and cubed, and
1 red pepper, cored, deseeded and cubed, and cook
over a medium heat, stirring occasionally, for 5 minutes
until the onion is softened but not browned. Add 6
tablespoons water and stir again. Cover and simmer
very gently for 5 minutes, or until the sweet potato
is tender. Add ½ teaspoon ground paprika and toss
again, then stir in 200 ml (7 fl oz) cashew cream and
4 tablespoons chopped flat leaf parsley and heat for
1–2 minutes over a gentle heat until piping hot but not
boiling, otherwise the cream may separate. Season well
with salt and pepper and serve on a bed of rice.

tindori & green mango curry

Serves **4**

Preparation time **20 minutes**

Cooking time **35 minutes**

125 g (4 oz) **dried green lentils**, rinsed and drained

1 small **green mango**

1 small **red onion**, finely chopped

handful of chopped **coriander**

3 tablespoons **vegetable oil**

1 teaspoon **ground turmeric**

2 teaspoons **garam masala**

1 teaspoon **cumin seeds**

1 teaspoon **black onion seeds**

1 **red chilli**, finely chopped

1 **green chilli,** finely chopped

3 large **tomatoes**, chopped

250 g (8 oz) **tindori**, rinsed, drained and trimmed

2 tablespoons **soft light brown sugar**

1 tablespoon **tamarind paste**

150 ml (¼ pint) **boiling water**

salt and **pepper**

chapatis, to serve

Cook the lentils in a saucepan of boiling water for 20 minutes until soft. Drain well.

Meanwhile, peel and stone the mango, then shred the flesh finely and mix with the onion and coriander. Cover and chill until required.

Heat the oil in a large saucepan, add the turmeric, garam masala, cumin seeds and black onion seeds and cook for 1–2 minutes until the spices are sizzling and the mustard seeds begin to pop.

Stir the chillies, tomatoes, tindori and cooked lentils into the spice mixture, then cover and simmer gently, stirring occasionally, for 10 minutes. Mix the brown sugar and tamarind paste with the measurement boiling water in a jug and add to the pan. Stir well and simmer for a further 5 minutes. Season with salt and pepper, then serve topped with the green mango and red onion mixture, along with chapatis.

turkish stuffed butternut squash

Serves **4**

Preparation time **25 minutes**

Cooking time **1 hour
5 minutes**

2 **butternut squash**, halved
and deseeded
4 tablespoons **olive oil**
salt and **pepper**

Filling
3 tablespoons **olive oil**
1 large **onion**, finely chopped
1 **garlic clove**, thinly sliced
1 teaspoon **ground cumin**
450 g (14½ oz) **tomatoes**,
roughly chopped
4 tablespoons chopped **flat
leaf parsley**
1 tablespoon chopped
oregano
2 tablespoons **sun-dried
tomato paste**
1 teaspoon **cumin seeds**
salt and **pepper**

Sit the squash halves, cut-side up, in a large roasting tin,
brush each with 1 tablespoon oil and season with salt
and pepper. Roast in a preheated oven, 220°C (425°F),
Gas Mark 7, for 45 minutes until lightly charred on top.

Meanwhile, heat the oil for the filling in a large, heavy-
based frying pan, add the onion, garlic and cumin and
cook over a medium-high heat, stirring occasionally,
for 4–5 minutes until beginning to soften. Add the
tomatoes, parsley, oregano and sun-dried tomato paste
and cook, stirring occasionally, for a further 5 minutes.
Season well with salt and pepper.

Divide the filling between the cavities of the roasted
squash halves and scatter with the cumin seeds.
Reduce the oven temperature to 180°C (350°F), Gas
Mark 4, and roast the stuffed squash for 20 minutes,
or until the filling is soft and golden in places. Serve with
a simple rocket salad if liked.

For Turkish stuffed peppers with raisins, heat
4 tablespoons olive oil in a large frying pan, add 2
roughly chopped onions, 2 thinly sliced garlic cloves and
2 teaspoons ground cumin and cook over a medium-
high heat, stirring occasionally, for about 8 minutes
until the onions are soft. Stir in 750 g (1½ lb) roughly
chopped tomatoes, 5 tablespoons raisins, 4 tablespoons
chopped flat leaf parsley and 2 tablespoons sun-
dried tomato paste, then cover and cook for a further
5 minutes. Season with salt and pepper. Fill 4 cored,
deseeded and halved peppers with the mixture in a
roasting tin, cover with foil and bake in a preheated
oven, 180°C (350°F), Gas Mark 4, for 20 minutes.
Remove the foil and cook for a further 10 minutes.

chunky tomato & bean stew

Serves **4**

Preparation time **15 minutes**

Cooking time **25 minutes**

2 tablespoons **olive oil**

1 **red onion**, chopped

1 **carrot**, peeled and cut into
chunks

2 **garlic cloves**, crushed

1 **courgette**, trimmed and cut
into chunks

1 **red chilli**, deseeded and
chopped

2 teaspoons chopped **thyme
leaves**

2 teaspoons **smoked paprika**

425 g (14 oz) can **mixed
beans in chilli sauce**

400 g (13 oz) can **chickpeas**,
drained

400 g (13 oz) can **chopped
tomatoes**

150 ml (¼ pint) **vegetable
stock**

salt and **pepper**

vegan tortilla chips, to serve

Heat the oil in a saucepan, add the onion and carrot
and cook over a gentle heat for 5 minutes until
softened. Stir in the garlic, courgette, chilli, thyme and
smoked paprika and cook for a further 5 minutes.

Stir the beans with their sauce, chickpeas, tomatoes
and stock into the pan. Bring to the boil, then simmer for
10 minutes until the vegetables are tender and the stew
has thickened slightly. Season with salt and pepper and
serve hot, with vegan tortilla chips.

For chunky tomato, bean & rice pot, heat 2
tablespoons olive oil in a saucepan, add 1 chopped
onion, 1 cored, deseeded and chopped green pepper,
1 peeled and chopped carrot, 1 trimmed and chopped
courgette, 2 crushed garlic cloves and 1 chopped red
chilli and cook over a medium heat for 5 minutes. Add
a 425 g (14 oz) can mixed beans in chilli sauce, a
400 g (13 oz) can chopped tomatoes, 200 ml (7 fl oz)
vegetable stock and 2 teaspoons each chopped thyme
leaves and smoked paprika. Bring to the boil, then stir
in 150 g (5 oz) long-grain rice and simmer for 10–12
minutes until the rice and vegetables are tender. Season
with salt and pepper and serve with a crisp green salad.

asian-style risotto

Serves **4**

Preparation time **15 minutes**

Cooking time **25 minutes**

1.2 litres (2 pints) **vegetable stock**

1 tablespoon **dark soy sauce**

2 tablespoons **mirin**

3 tablespoons **sunflower oil**

1 tablespoon **sesame oil**

bunch of **spring onions**, thickly sliced

2 **garlic cloves**, chopped

2.5 cm (1 inch) piece of **fresh root ginger**, peeled and grated

375 g (12 oz) **Arborio rice**

6 **kaffir lime leaves**

250 g (8 oz) **shiitake mushrooms**, wiped and stalks discarded

15 g (½ oz) chopped **coriander**, plus extra sprigs to garnish

Bring the stock, soy sauce and mirin to a simmer in a saucepan. Meanwhile, heat 2 tablespoons of the sunflower oil and the sesame oil in a separate saucepan, add the spring onions, garlic and ginger and cook over a high heat, stirring, for 1 minute. Stir in the rice and lime leaves and cook over a low heat for 1 minute until glossy.

Stir 150 ml (¼ pint) of the stock mixture into the rice and simmer, stirring, until it is almost all absorbed. Add the stock, a little at a time, and simmer, stirring, until all but a ladleful has been absorbed. Meanwhile, slice all but a few of the mushrooms. Heat the remaining oil in a frying pan, add the mushrooms and cook over a medium heat, stirring frequently, for 5 minutes until golden.

Add the coriander to the risotto with the sliced mushrooms and the remaining stock. Simmer, stirring frequently, until almost all the stock is absorbed and the rice is tender and cooked through. Serve garnished with the whole mushrooms and coriander sprigs.

For coconut & chilli risotto, heat 2 tablespoons oil in a saucepan, add 1 roughly chopped leek, 1 sliced red pepper, 1 chopped garlic clove and 1 finely chopped red chilli and cook, stirring, over a medium heat for 4 minutes until softened. Stir in 300 g (10 oz) Arborio rice and 6 kaffir lime leaves, then pour in 300 ml (½ pint) vegan stock. Bring to the boil, then simmer, stirring, until the liquid is almost all absorbed. Add 400 ml (14 fl oz) coconut milk with another 150 ml (¼ pint) stock and simmer, stirring frequently, for a further 15 minutes until the liquid is almost all absorbed and the rice is tender. Stir in 200 g (7 oz) frozen sweetcorn with the grated rind of 1 lime and heat through. Scatter with chopped coriander.

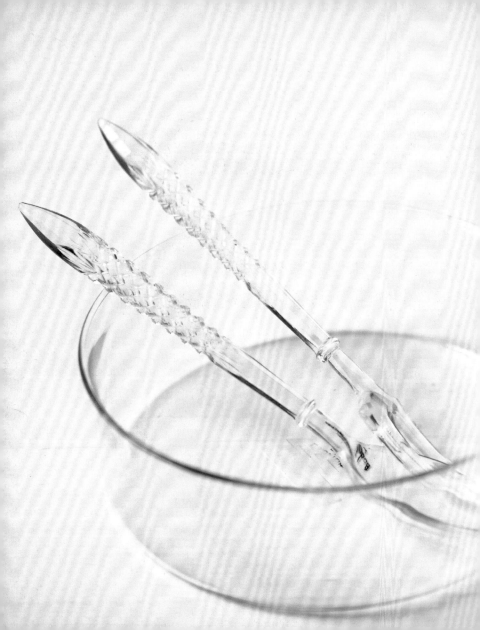

salads &
sides

spinach & butternut salad

Serves **4**

Preparation time **20 minutes**

Cooking time **30 minutes**

625 g (1¼ lb) **butternut squash**, peeled, deseeded and cut into wedges

2 tablespoons **flaxseed (linseed) oil**

125 g (4 oz) **walnut halves**

1 tablespoon **maple syrup**

pinch of **sea salt flakes**

125 g (4 oz) **baby spinach leaves**

salt and **pepper**

Mustard dressing

1 tablespoon **white wine vinegar**

1 teaspoon **wholegrain mustard**

3 tablespoons **olive oil**

pinch of **caster sugar**

salt and **pepper**

Toss the butternut squash with the flaxseed oil on a baking sheet and season with salt and pepper. Spread out in a single layer and roast in a preheated oven, 200°C (400°F), Gas Mark 6, for 30 minutes until tender and beginning to char in places.

Meanwhile, mix the walnuts and maple syrup together in a small bowl and spread out over a separate baking sheet lined with foil. Sprinkle with the salt flakes and bake in the oven for 5–7 minutes until toasted and caramelized.

Put all the dressing ingredients in a screw-top jar and season with salt and pepper. Screw on the lid and shake well to mix.

Transfer the roasted squash to a salad bowl and add the spinach. Pour over the dressing and toss gently together. Sprinkle over the caramelized walnuts.

For chicory, roasted pear & caramelized pecan salad, peel, core and thickly slice 3 pears. Toss with 2 tablespoons flaxseed (linseed) oil on a baking sheet, spread out in a single layer and roast in a preheated oven, 200°C (400°F), Gas Mark 6, for 20 minutes until tender. Meanwhile, mix 125 g (4 oz) pecan halves and 1 tablespoon maple syrup together in a small bowl. Spread out over a separate baking sheet lined with foil, sprinkle with a pinch of sea salt flakes and bake in the oven for 5–7 minutes until toasted and caramelized. Prepare the mustard dressing as above. Put the leaves from 2 heads of chicory in a serving dish. Top with the roasted pears, drizzle over 4 tablespoons of the mustard dressing and sprinkle over the caramelized pecans.

roasted roots & quinoa salad

Serves **4**
Preparation time **10 minutes**
Cooking time **35–40 minutes**

300 g (10 oz) **raw baby
  beetroot**, scrubbed, halved
  or quartered if large
300 g (10 oz) **baby carrots**,
  scrubbed
1 tablespoon **olive oil**
1 teaspoon **cumin seeds**
150 g (5 oz) **quinoa**, rinsed
  and drained
400 g (13 oz) can **chickpeas**,
  drained
1 small **red onion**, thinly sliced
small handful of **mint leaves**,
  roughly chopped
2 tablespoons **blanched
  hazelnuts**, roughly chopped
juice of **1 lime**
1 tablespoon **tamari** or **soy
  sauce**
1 teaspoon **sesame oil**
salt and **pepper**

Put the beetroot and carrots in a roasting tin. Drizzle over the olive oil, sprinkle with the cumin seeds and season well with salt and pepper, then toss until the roots are evenly coated in the oil. Roast in a preheated oven, 200°C (400°F), Gas Mark 6, for 30–35 minutes until tender.

Meanwhile, cook the quinoa in a saucepan of boiling water for 10–12 minutes until tender, then drain. Tip into a large bowl, add the chickpeas, onion, mint and hazelnuts and toss together.

Mix the lime juice, tamari or soy sauce and sesame oil together in a jug, pour over the quinoa mixture and gently toss together. Add the roasted beetroots and carrots and lightly mix through.

For roasted carrot & parsnip salad with edamame beans, toss 300 g (10 oz) each of scrubbed baby carrots and baby parsnips with 1 tablespoon olive oil, 1 teaspoon cumin seeds and salt and pepper in a roasting tin. Roast in a preheated oven, 200°C (400°F), Gas Mark 6, for 20–25 minutes until tender. Meanwhile, cook the quinoa as above, adding 125 g (4 oz) frozen edamame (soya) beans for the final 3 minutes of the cooking time. Drain and tip into a large bowl. Add 1 thinly sliced red onion, a handful of roughly chopped flat leaf parsley and 2 tablespoons toasted blanched almonds, roughly chopped. Make the lime juice dressing as above, pour over the quinoa mixture and gently toss together. Add the roasted carrots and parsnips and lightly mix through.

new potato, basil & pine nut salad

Serves **4–6**

Preparation time **10 minutes**, plus cooling

Cooking time **15–18 minutes**

1 kg (2 lb) **new potatoes**, scrubbed

4 tablespoons **extra virgin olive oil**

1½ tablespoons **white wine vinegar**

50 g (2 oz) **pine nuts**

½ bunch of **basil leaves**

salt and **pepper**

Cook the potatoes in a large saucepan of lightly salted boiling water for 12–15 minutes until tender. Drain well and transfer to a large bowl. Cut any large potatoes in half.

Whisk together the oil, vinegar and a little salt and pepper in a jug. Add half to the potatoes, stir well and leave to cool completely.

Toast the pine nuts in a dry frying pan over a medium heat, shaking the pan occasionally, for 2–3 minutes until golden. Tip out of the pan and leave to cool.

Add the toasted pine nuts, the remaining dressing and basil to the potatoes, toss well and then serve.

broccoli, pea & avocado salad

Serves **4**

Preparation time **20 minutes**, plus cooling

Cooking time **5 minutes**

1 tablespoon **sesame seeds**

1 tablespoon **chia seeds**

350 g (11½ oz) **broccoli**, cut into small florets

150 g (5 oz) **frozen peas**

1 large ripe **avocado**, peeled, stoned and chopped

125 g (4 oz) **baby spinach leaves**

25 g (1 oz) **sprouting alfalfa**

2 tablespoons chopped **mint**

juice of 1 **lime**

2 teaspoons **sesame oil**

1.5 cm (¾ inch) piece of **fresh root ginger**, peeled and grated

salt and **pepper**

Toast the sesame and chia seeds in a dry pan over a medium heat, shaking the pan a couple of times, for 30 seconds until golden. Tip out of the pan and leave to cool.

Blanch the broccoli with the peas in a large saucepan of boiling water for 2 minutes until the broccoli is just tender but still firm. Drain, rinse under cold water and drain again.

Tip the broccoli and peas into a large salad bowl. Add the avocado, spinach leaves, alfalfa, mint and toasted seeds.

Whisk the lime juice, oil and ginger together in a jug and season with salt and pepper. Pour over the salad and toss well to mix.

For spinach, beetroot & pomegranate salad, toast the sesame and chia seeds as above. Put 125 g (4 oz) baby spinach leaves in a salad bowl with 175 g (6 oz) chopped Sweetfire beetroot (cooked beetroot infused with a sweet chilli marinade), 2 sliced celery sticks, 1 large ripe avocado, peeled, stoned and chopped, 25 g (1 oz) sprouting alfalfa, small handful of chopped flat leaf parsley leaves and the toasted seeds. Make the lime juice dressing as above, then pour over the salad and toss well to mix.

warm lentil, tomato & onion salad

Serves **4**
Preparation time **15 minutes**
Cooking time **40–45 minutes**

1 tablespoon **olive oil**
1 large **red onion**, thinly sliced
50 g (2 oz) **fresh root ginger**,
   peeled and chopped
4 **garlic cloves**, thinly sliced
125 g (4 oz) **dried green
   lentils**, rinsed and drained
100 g (3½ oz) **dried red split
   lentils**, rinsed and drained
½ teaspoon **ground cinnamon**
400 g (13 oz) fresh **tomatoes**,
   roughly chopped, or
   400 g (13 oz) can **chopped
   tomatoes**
350 ml (12 fl oz) **water** or
   vegetable stock
2 teaspoons **black onion
   seeds**
salt and **pepper**
parsley leaves, to garnish

Heat the oil in a large, heavy-based saucepan, add the onion, ginger and garlic and cook over a gentle heat, stirring frequently, for 10 minutes until softened but not coloured.

Stir the lentils, cinnamon, tomatoes and measurement water or stock into the pan, season with salt and pepper and bring to the boil. Cover and simmer gently for 30–35 minutes, or until the lentils are tender and the liquid is absorbed.

Spoon the lentils into warmed serving bowls, sprinkle with the black onion seeds and garnish with parsley leaves. Serve warm with lemon wedges and toasted wholemeal flatbreads if liked.

For no-cook lentil, tomato & onion salad, rinse and drain a 250 g (8 oz) pack cooked lentils. Put in a bowl and mix with ½ finely chopped red onion, 4 chopped tomatoes, 1 small crushed garlic clove, 1 cm (½ inch) piece of fresh root ginger, peeled and grated, and 2 tablespoons chopped flat leaf parsley. Whisk 2 tablespoons lemon juice, 1 tablespoon olive oil and a pinch each of ground cinnamon and paprika together in a jug and season with salt and pepper. Add the dressing to the lentil salad and toss to coat, then serve garnished with parsley leaves.

tamarind-dressed chinese salad

Serves **4**
Preparation time **20 minutes**

½ head of **Chinese leaf,**
 trimmed and finely shredded
200 g (7 oz) **mooli**, peeled
 and grated
200 g (7 oz) **carrots**, peeled
 and grated
¼ **cucumber**, halved
 lengthways and thinly sliced
8 **spring onions**, diagonally
 thinly sliced
1 **mango**, peeled, stoned and
 cut into chunks
125 g (4 oz) **raw unsalted
 cashew nuts**, toasted
handful of **coriander leaves**

Dressing
8 tablespoons **boiling water**
2 tablespoons **tamarind paste**
1 tablespoon **palm** or
 demerara sugar
1 **red chilli**, thinly sliced
4 tablespoons **light soy sauce**
finely grated rind and juice of
 1 **lime**

Put the Chinese leaf in a large bowl with the grated mooli and carrots and toss well to mix.

Add the cucumber, spring onions and mango to the bowl and toss again, then scatter over the cashews and coriander leaves and give a final toss.

Pour the measurement boiling water over the tamarind paste in a small jug and blend together with the back of a spoon until well mixed and the paste is dissolved. Add the sugar and stir until dissolved. Whisk in the chilli, soy sauce and lime rind and juice. Pour over the salad and toss well before serving.

For Thai peanut salad with chilli & soy dressing,

toss ½ head of Chinese leaf, trimmed and finely shredded, with 200 g (7 oz) bean sprouts, 1 cored, deseeded and finely sliced red pepper, ¼ cucumber, halved lengthways and thinly sliced, 1 peeled and grated carrot and 8 spring onions, diagonally thinly sliced, in a large bowl. Add 150 g (5 oz) salted peanuts and toss again. Whisk together 3 tablespoons light soy sauce, 2 tablespoons sesame oil, 3 tablespoons chopped coriander and 1 finely chopped red chilli in a jug. Pour over the salad and toss well before serving.

mediterranean potato salad

Serves **4**

Preparation time **10 minutes**,
  plus cooling

Cooking time **20 minutes**

450 g (14½ oz) **potatoes**,
  peeled and cut into chunks

pinch of **saffron threads**

125 g (4 oz) **sunblush
  tomatoes**, halved

75 g (3 oz) **pitted black
  olives**, roughly chopped

6 tablespoons **olive oil**

4 tablespoons **chia seeds**

5 tablespoons chopped **basil
  leaves**

3 tablespoons **capers**

salt and **pepper**

Pour over just enough cold water to cover the potatoes
in a saucepan and add the saffron. Bring to the boil,
then cover and simmer very gently for 15 minutes until
tender and cooked through. Drain and leave to cool.

Put the sunblush tomatoes, olives, oil, chia seeds,
basil leaves and capers in a large bowl, add the cooled
potatoes and gently toss together. Season with a little
salt and plenty of pepper.

Divide the salad between 4 serving bowls and serve
with fresh crusty bread or a simple rocket salad if liked.

For Mediterranean pasta salad, cook 225 g (7½ oz)
dried pasta shapes in a large saucepan of lightly salted
boiling water for 8–10 minutes until just tender. Drain
well, rinse under cold water and drain again. Put 125 g
(4 oz) roughly chopped sunblush tomatoes, 75 g (3 oz)
roughly chopped pitted black olives, 6 tablespoons olive
oil, 4 tablespoons chia seeds, 5 tablespoons chopped
basil leaves and 3 tablespoons capers in a large bowl.
Toss well so that all the ingredients are well mixed.
Season with salt and pepper before serving.

fennel, apple & red cabbage slaw

Serves **4**
Preparation time **20 minutes**

¼ **red cabbage**, shredded
1 **fennel bulb**, trimmed and
    thinly sliced
1 **dessert apple**, cored and
    thinly sliced
1 small **red onion**, thinly sliced
1 **celery stick**, sliced
2 tablespoons **sunflower
    seeds**
2 tablespoons **pumpkin
    seeds**
5 tablespoons **vegan
    mayonnaise**
1 tablespoon **lemon juice**
1 teaspoon **Dijon mustard**
small handful of **flat leaf
    parsley**, roughly chopped
salt and **pepper**

Put the cabbage in a large bowl, add the fennel, apple, onion, celery and sunflower and pumpkin seeds and toss well to combine.

Mix the mayonnaise, lemon juice and mustard together in a small bowl and season with salt and pepper. Add to the cabbage mixture with the parsley and gently toss together to coat in the dressing.

For beetroot & celeriac slaw with horseradish dressing, coarsely grate 1 peeled raw beetroot, 150 g (5 oz) peeled celeriac and 1 peeled and cored apple into a bowl. Add ¼ shredded red cabbage, 1 small red onion, thinly sliced, and 2 tablespoons each sunflower and pumpkin seeds. Mix 3 tablespoons vegan mayonnaise, 1 tablespoon lemon juice and 1 teaspoon grated horseradish together in a small bowl and season with salt and pepper. Add to the vegetables with a small handful of roughly chopped flat leaf parsley and toss well to mix.

roasted summer vegetables

Serves **4**

Preparation time **15 minutes**

Cooking time **45–50 minutes**

1 **red pepper**, cored, deseeded and thickly sliced

1 **yellow pepper**, cored, deseeded and thickly sliced

1 **aubergine**, trimmed and cut into chunks

2 **yellow** or **green courgettes**, trimmed and cut into chunks

1 **red onion**, cut into wedges

6 **garlic cloves**, peeled

2 tablespoons **extra virgin rapeseed** or **olive oil**

4–5 **thyme sprigs**

150 g (5 oz) **mixed yellow** and **red baby plum tomatoes**

150 g (5 oz) **hazelnuts**

125 g (4 oz) **rocket leaves**

2 tablespoons **raspberry** or **balsamic vinegar**

salt and **pepper**

handful of **mustard cress**, to garnish (optional)

Toss all the vegetables, except the tomatoes, and the garlic cloves in a large bowl with the oil. Season with a little salt and pepper and add the thyme. Tip into a large roasting tin and roast in a preheated oven, 190°C (375°F), Gas Mark 5, for 40–45 minutes, or until the vegetables are tender. Add the tomatoes and return to the oven for a further 5 minutes, or until the tomatoes are just softened and beginning to burst.

Meanwhile, tip the hazelnuts into a small roasting tin and toast in the oven for about 10–12 minutes, or until golden and the skins are peeling away. Leave to cool, then rub off the excess skin with a clean tea towel and lightly crush the nuts.

Toss the rocket leaves gently with the roasted vegetables and heap on to large plates. Scatter over the crushed hazelnuts and drizzle with the vinegar. Scatter over the mustard cress, if using, and serve immediately.

For roasted vegetable pasta sauce, roast all the vegetables, except the tomatoes, and the garlic cloves as above, then tip into a saucepan with the tomatoes, 500 ml (17 fl oz) passata and 150 ml (¼ pint) vegetable stock. Bring to the boil, then simmer gently for 20 minutes. Remove from the heat and use a stick blender to blend until smooth. Season with salt and pepper and serve over cooked pasta.

marinated tofu with crunchy salad

Serves **4**

Preparation time **20 minutes**,
  plus marinating

Cooking time **10 minutes**

225 g (7 ½ oz) **firm tofu**,
  drained

3 tablespoons **light soy sauce**

1 tablespoon **hoisin sauce**

1 tablespoon **sesame oil**

2 tablespoons chopped
  coriander

1 small **red chilli**, deseeded
  and finely chopped

2.5 cm (1 inch) piece of **fresh
  root ginger**, peeled and
  grated

175 g (6 oz) **bean sprouts**

6 **spring onions**, cut into
  strips

¼ head of **Chinese leaf**,
  trimmed and finely shredded

6 tablespoons **salted peanuts**

Cut the tofu into 2.5 cm (1 inch) cubes, put in a bowl
with 1 tablespoon of the soy sauce, the hoisin sauce,
sesame oil, coriander, chilli and ginger and gently toss
to mix. Cover and leave to marinate in the refrigerator
for 2 hours or overnight.

Put the bean sprouts, spring onions, Chinese leaf
and peanuts in a large bowl and toss well. Add the
remaining 2 tablespoons soy sauce and toss to
lightly coat.

Heat a griddle pan until hot, add the marinated tofu
and cook over a high heat, turning occasionally, for
2–3 minutes until lightly scorched on all sides. Toss
into the salad ingredients and serve.

For oriental tofu with sesame seeds, cut 225 g
(7 ½ oz) drained firm tofu into 4 thin slices and marinate
as above. Remove from the marinade to a plate and
scatter 2 teaspoons sesame seeds over both sides of
the tofu slices. Heat a griddle pan until hot, add the tofu
and cook over a medium heat for 1–2 minutes on each
side until scorched. Toss 125 g (4 oz) bean sprouts and
2 thinly sliced spring onions with 1 tablespoon dark
soy sauce in a bowl, then divide between 4 small plates
and top with the hot tofu. Sprinkle with 1 tablespoon
chopped coriander and serve as a salad starter.

asparagus with sesame dressing

Serves **4**
Preparation time **15 minutes**
Cooking time **15 minutes**

3 bunches of **asparagus**
  spears, trimmed
4 tablespoons **olive oil**

Dressing
4 tablespoons **sesame seeds**
4 tablespoons **tahini**
finely grated rind and juice of
  1 **lemon**
3 tablespoons **light soy sauce**
2 tablespoons **mirin**
4 tablespoons **water**

Lay the asparagus spears in a roasting tin, drizzle with 2 tablespoons of the oil and toss until evenly coated in the oil. Roast in a preheated oven, 220°C (425°F), Gas Mark 7, for 15 minutes until tender and lightly charred in places.

Meanwhile, toast the sesame seeds in a dry frying pan over a medium heat, shaking the pan occasionally, for about 2 minutes until golden. Transfer to a jug with the tahini, lemon rind and juice, soy sauce, mirin and the measurement water. Add the remaining olive oil then use a stick blender to blend until smooth.

Spoon half the dressing over the roasted asparagus and toss well to coat. Arrange on 4 serving plates and serve the remaining dressing separately.

For roasted baby carrots with tahini & sesame dip, put 350 g (11½ oz) scrubbed baby carrots in a roasting tin, drizzle over 1 tablespoon olive oil and toss until evenly coated in the oil. Roast in a preheated oven, 220°C (425°F), Gas Mark 7, for 20 minutes until just tender and lightly charred in places. To make the dip, put 4 tablespoons tahini into a jug with the finely grated rind of 1 lemon and 2 tablespoons each light soy sauce and toasted sesame seeds. Use a stick blender to blend until smooth. Transfer to a small serving bowl and place on a serving platter. Arrange the roasted carrots around the bowl for dipping, once cool enough to handle.

pepper & aubergine hummus

Serves **4–6**
Preparation time **10 minutes**,
   plus cooling
Cooking time **50 minutes**

1 **red pepper**, cored,
   deseeded and quartered
3 **garlic cloves**, unpeeled and
   lightly crushed
1 **aubergine**, trimmed and cut
   into large chunks
1 tablespoon **chilli oil**, plus
   extra to serve
½ tablespoon **fennel seeds**
   (optional)
400 g (13 oz) can **chickpeas**,
   drained
1 tablespoon **tahini**
1 teaspoon **sesame seeds**,
   lightly toasted
salt and **pepper**

To serve
4 **wholemeal pitta breads**
olive oil spray
1 teaspoon **paprika**
salt

Arrange the red pepper, garlic cloves and aubergine in a single layer in a large roasting tin. Drizzle with the chilli oil, sprinkle with the fennel seeds, if using, and season with salt and pepper. Roast in a preheated oven, 190°C (375°F), Gas Mark 5, for 35–40 minutes, or until softened and golden. Remove from the oven but do not turn it off.

Squeeze the soft garlic out of its skin and put in a blender or food processor with the roasted vegetables, three-quarters of the chickpeas and the tahini. Blend until almost smooth, season with salt and pepper and then spoon into a serving bowl. Cover with clingfilm and leave to cool.

Cut the pitta breads into 2.5 cm (1 inch) strips and put in a large bowl. Spray with a little olive oil and toss with the paprika and a little salt until well coated. Spread out in a single layer on a baking sheet. Toast in the oven for 10–12 minutes, or until crisp.

Sprinkle the hummus with the remaining chickpeas and the sesame seeds and drizzle with 1–2 tablespoons chilli oil. Serve with the toasted pitta breads.

For roasted artichoke & pepper hummus, roast the red pepper and garlic cloves as above with a drained 400 g (13 oz) can artichoke hearts in water instead of the aubergine, using 1 tablespoon lemon-infused oil in place of the chilli oil and omitting the fennel seeds. Continue with the recipe above to make the hummus and toast the pitta breads.

mushrooms with salsa verde

Serves **4**

Preparation time **20 minutes**

Cooking time **10 minutes**

1 tablespoon **red wine vinegar**

1 teaspoon **sugar**

finely grated rind and juice of 1 **lemon**

5 tablespoons **olive oil**

1 **garlic clove**, finely chopped

2 tablespoons chopped **parsley**

2 tablespoons chopped **basil**

1 tablespoon **capers**, finely chopped

4 **portobello mushrooms**, trimmed

salt and **pepper**

4 slices of **walnut bread**, lightly toasted, to serve

Put the vinegar in a small bowl with the sugar, lemon rind and juice, 2 tablespoons of the oil, the garlic, parsley, basil and capers. Mix together well and season with a little salt and plenty of pepper.

Heat the remaining 3 tablespoons oil in a large, heavy-based frying pan, add the mushrooms and cook over a high heat, turning once, for 5–6 minutes until softened.

Turn the mushrooms out on to 4 small warmed serving plates, spoon over the salsa verde and serve with toasted walnut bread.

For roasted peppers with salsa verde, cut 2 red peppers in half lengthways and remove the core and seeds but keep the stalk intact. Place the pepper halves, cut-side down, in a roasting tin, drizzle with 1 tablespoon olive oil and roast in a preheated oven, 200°C (400°F), Gas Mark 6, for 20–25 minutes until soft. Make the salsa verde as above and spoon over the roasted peppers on 4 small warmed serving plates. Serve with lightly toasted Mediterranean bread.

onion bhajis with mango chutney

Serves **4**
Preparation time **20 minutes**
Cooking time **15 minutes**

2 teaspoons **cumin seeds**,
   toasted
½ teaspoon **ground turmeric**
1 teaspoon **ground coriander**
small handful of **coriander
   leaves**, roughly chopped
1 **green chilli**, deseeded and
   finely chopped
250 g (8 oz) **onions**, halved
   and sliced
150 g (5 oz) **gram (chickpea)
   flour**
vegetable oil, for deep-frying

Chutney
1 large ripe **mango**, peeled
   and stoned
½ **red chilli**, deseeded
1 teaspoon **black onion
   seeds**, toasted
1 teaspoon **light muscovado
   sugar**
1 teaspoon **white wine
   vinegar**
2 teaspoons **rapeseed oil**
½ teaspoon **ground coriander**
leaves from a few **mint sprigs**
salt and **pepper**

Pulse all the chutney ingredients, except the seasoning, together in a food processor until finely chopped. Season with salt and pepper and transfer to a serving bowl.

Put the cumin seeds, turmeric, ground and fresh coriander, chilli and onions in a bowl. Stir to mix, then sprinkle over the flour and add enough cold water to bind the mixture together. The mixture needs to be thick enough to hold its shape in spoonfuls.

Half-fill a deep pan with vegetable oil and heat to 180–190°C (350–375°F), or until a cube of bread browns in 30 seconds. Drop spoonfuls of the mixture about the size of a golf ball, in batches, into the oil and fry for 3–4 minutes until golden and crisp. Remove from the pan with a slotted spoon, drain on kitchen paper and keep warm in a low oven. Serve warm with the chutney.

For cabbage & parsnip bhajis with coconut mango chutney, pulse together 1 large ripe mango, peeled and stoned, 2 tablespoons coarsely grated fresh coconut or 1 tablespoon unsweetened desiccated coconut, ½ deseeded red chilli, 2 teaspoons rapeseed oil, 1 teaspoon each light muscovado sugar, black onion seeds and white wine vinegar, ½ teaspoon ground coriander and a few coriander leaves in a food processor until finely chopped. Season with salt and pepper and transfer to a bowl. Mix together 2 teaspoons each toasted cumin seeds and garam masala, 2 tablespoons roughly chopped coriander leaves, 1 chopped green chilli, 75 g (3 oz) shredded cabbage and 175 g (6 oz) peeled and coarsely grated parsnip in a bowl. Sprinkle over 150 g (5 oz) gram (chickpea) flour and continue as above to make and deep-fry the bhajis. Serve with the chutney.

bean, lemon & rosemary hummus

Serves **4–6**
Preparation time **10 minutes,**
  plus cooling
Cooking time **10 minutes**

6 tablespoons **extra virgin
  olive oil,** plus extra to serve
4 **shallots,** finely chopped
2 large **garlic cloves,** crushed
1 teaspoon chopped
  rosemary, plus extra sprigs
  to garnish
finely grated rind and juice of
  ½ **lemon**
2 x 400 g (13 oz) cans **butter
  beans,** drained
salt and **pepper**
toasted **ciabatta,** to serve

Heat the oil in a frying pan, add the shallots, garlic,
chopped rosemary and lemon rind and cook over a
gentle heat, stirring occasionally, for 10 minutes until
the shallots are softened. Leave to cool.

Transfer the shallot mixture to a blender or food
processor, add all the remaining ingredients and blend
until smooth.

Spread the hummus on to toasted ciabatta, garnish
with rosemary sprigs and serve drizzled with oil.

For chickpea & chilli dip, put 2 x 400 g (13 oz) cans
chickpeas, drained, 2 deseeded and chopped red
chillies, 1 large garlic clove, crushed, 2 tablespoons
lemon juice and salt and pepper in a blender or food
processor and add enough extra virgin olive oil to blend
to a soft paste. Serve as a dip with vegetable crudités.

breads & baking

chilli & courgette foccacia

Serves **6**

Preparation time **30 minutes**, plus proving

Cooking time **30–35 minutes**

500 g (1 lb) **strong white bread flour**, plus extra for dusting

7 g (¼ oz) sachet **fast-action dried yeast**

1 teaspoon **salt**

4 tablespoons **olive oil**, plus extra for oiling

275 ml (9 fl oz) **warm water**

½ small **onion**, thinly sliced

½ small **courgette**, trimmed and thinly sliced

1 **red chilli**, deseeded and thinly sliced

1 teaspoon **sea salt flakes**

a few small **rosemary sprigs**

Sift the flour into a bowl. Add the yeast to one side and the salt to the other side. Add 2 tablespoons of the oil and the measurement water and mix to form a dough, adding a little more water if the dough seems dry.

Tip the dough on to a lightly floured surface and knead for 10 minutes until smooth and stretchy. Put the dough in a clean bowl, cover with clingfilm and leave to rise in a warm place for about 1 hour until doubled in size.

Turn the dough out on to a lightly floured surface and knead lightly for 1 minute. Press or roll the dough out to a rough oblong about 1 cm (½ inch) thick and place on a lightly oiled baking sheet. Loosely cover and leave to prove for 20 minutes.

Meanwhile, heat 1 tablespoon of the remaining oil in a frying pan, add the onion and cook over a medium heat for about 3 minutes until just softened. Add the courgette and chilli and cook for a further 3 minutes. Set aside.

Press indentations with your fingertip into the dough surface. Drizzle over the remaining oil and bake in a preheated oven, 200°C (400°F), Gas Mark 6, for 10 minutes. Scatter over the vegetable mixture with the salt flakes and rosemary sprigs and bake for a further 10–15 minutes until golden. Cool on a wire rack.

For potato, onion & thyme focaccia, make the dough as above. While it is proving, fry 1 small sliced onion and 1 large baking potato, scrubbed and thinly sliced, in 1 tablespoon oil over a medium heat for 5–8 minutes until tender. Bake as above, adding the onion and potato slices instead of the vegetable mixture, and adding thyme sprigs instead of rosemary.

olive & tomato bread

Makes **1 large loaf**
Preparation time **1¾–2¾
hours**, depending on
machine, plus proving
Cooking time **30 minutes**

Dough
275 ml (9 fl oz) **water**
2 tablespoons **olive oil**, plus
extra for oiling
1 teaspoon **salt**
475 g (15 oz) **strong white
bread flour**, plus extra for
dusting
1 teaspoon **caster sugar**
1¼ teaspoons **fast-action
dried yeast**

To finish
125 g (4 oz) pitted or stuffed
green olives, roughly
chopped
40 g (1½ oz) **sun-dried
tomatoes** (not in oil), roughly
chopped
sea salt flakes and **paprika**,
for sprinkling

Lift the bread pan out of a bread-making machine and
fit the blade. Put all the dough ingredients in the pan,
following the order specified in the machine's manual.

Fit the pan into the machine and close the lid. Set to the
dough programme.

Turn the dough out on to a lightly floured surface at the
end of the programme. Gradually work in the olives and
sun-dried tomatoes. Pat the dough into a 20 cm (8 inch)
round and use a floured knife to mark it into 8 wedges.
Do not cut right through to the base.

Sprinkle salt flakes and paprika over the dough,
transfer to a large, lightly oiled baking sheet, cover
loosely with oiled clingfilm and leave to rise in a warm
place for 30 minutes until it is half as big again.

Bake in a preheated oven, 200°C (400°F), Gas Mark 6,
for 30 minutes. Check after 15 minutes and cover with
foil if over-browning. Transfer to a wire rack to cool.

For paprika, Peppadew, black olive & rosemary
bread, prepare the bread dough as above, adding
2 teaspoons paprika to the flour. At the end of the
dough programme, turn the dough out on to a lightly
floured surface and knead in 50 g (2 oz) drained and
roughly chopped Peppadew peppers, 75 g (3 oz)
roughly chopped pitted black olives and 1 tablespoon
chopped rosemary. Pat into a round and mark into
wedges as above. Sprinkle with 1 teaspoon sea salt
flakes and transfer to a lightly oiled baking sheet. Leave
to rise, bake and cool as above.

herb & walnut rye soda bread

Serves **6**
Preparation time **15 minutes**,
  plus standing
Cooking time **40–45 minutes**

250 g (8 oz) **rye flour**
50 g (2 oz) **walnuts**, roughly
  chopped, plus 1 tablespoon
  roughly chopped for
  scattering
4 tablespoons chopped **mixed
  herbs**, such as rosemary,
  parsley or thyme
1 teaspoon **bicarbonate of
  soda**
2 teaspoons **xanthan gum**
¼ teaspoon **salt**
225 ml (7½ floz) **rice milk**
25 ml (1 fl oz) **rapeseed oil**,
  plus extra for oiling

Mix together the flour, walnuts, mixed herbs,
bicarbonate of soda, xanthan gum and salt in a large
bowl, then make a well in the centre. Whisk together the
rice milk and rapeseed oil in a jug, then pour into the
well and stir in with a wooden spoon until a soft, slightly
sticky dough is formed.

Turn the dough out on to a lightly floured surface and
pat into a 18 cm (7 inch) round. Place on to a baking
sheet. Scatter over the extra walnuts and gently press
to adhere to the dough. Make a deep cross in the dough
with a sharp knife, then leave to stand in a warm place
for 30 minutes.

Bake in a preheated oven, 220°C (425°F), Gas Mark
7, for 40–45 minutes until the bread is crisp on the
outside and cooked through – the base should sound
hollow when tapped with the fingertips. Turn out on to a
wire rack to cool before slicing thickly to serve.

For pumpkin & sunflower seed wholemeal soda
bread, mix together 250 g (8 oz) wholemeal plain
flour, 1 teaspoon bicarbonate of soda, 2 teaspoons
xanthan gum and 4 tablespoons each sunflower seeds
and pumpkin seeds in a large bowl. Make a well in
the centre. Continue with the recipe as above, adding
the rice milk and rapeseed oil to make a dough and
preparing it on the baking sheet for baking. After
cutting the cross in the dough, scatter with an extra
tablespoon pumpkin seeds and leave in a warm place
for 30 minutes. Bake, cool and serve as above.

pitta breads

Makes **8 breads**

Preparation time **1¾–2¾ hours**, depending on machine, plus proving

Cooking time **10–12 minutes**

250 ml (8 fl oz) **water**

1 tablespoon **olive oil**

1 teaspoon **salt**

½ teaspoon ground **cumin**

375 g (12 oz) **strong white bread flour**, plus extra for dusting

1 teaspoon **caster sugar**

1 teaspoon **fast-action dried yeast**

Lift the bread pan out of a bread-making machine and fit the blade. Put the ingredients in the pan, following the order specified in the machine's manual.

Fit the pan into the machine and close the lid. Set to the dough programme.

Turn the dough out on to a lightly floured surface at the end of the programme and cut it into 8 equal-sized pieces. Roll out each piece to an oval about 15 cm (6 inches) long. Arrange in a single layer on a well-floured clean, dry tea towel. Cover loosely with a second clean, dry tea towel and leave to rise in a warm place for 30 minutes.

Put a floured baking sheet in a preheated oven, 230°C (450°F), Gas Mark 8, and leave to heat up for 5 minutes. Transfer half the breads to the baking sheet and cook for 5–6 minutes until just beginning to colour. Remove from the oven and leave to cool on a wire rack while you cook the remainder. Wrap the warm pittas in a clean, dry tea towel to keep them soft until ready to serve. If they are left to go cold, warm the pittas through in a hot oven before serving.

For olive & herb mini pittas, make the dough as above, adding 50 g (2 oz) chopped pitted black olives and a large handful of chopped parsley and mint to the dough when the machine beeps. Turn the dough out on to a lightly floured surface at the end of the programme and cut it into 16 pieces. Roll out each piece thinly to an oval 10–12 cm (4–5 inches) long. Leave to rise and then bake as above.

mini parsnip & parsley loaves

Makes **10 loaves**
Preparation time **1¾–2¾ hours**, depending on machine, plus cooling and proving
Cooking time **20–25 minutes**

150 g (5 oz) small **parsnips**, peeled and cut into chunks
2 tablespoons **olive oil**, plus extra for oiling
large pinch of **saffron threads**, crumbled
1½ teaspoons **salt**
450 g (14½ oz) **strong white bread flour**, plus extra for dusting
1 teaspoon **caster sugar**
1¼ teaspoons **fast-action dried yeast**
4 tablespoons chopped **parsley**
1 medium-strength **red chilli**, deseeded and thinly sliced
soya or other non-dairy milk, for brushing

Cook the parsnips in a saucepan of boiling water for 10 minutes until just tender. Drain, reserving the liquid, return to the pan and mash. Leave to cool.

Measure 275 ml (9 fl oz) of the reserved cooking liquid. Lift the bread pan out of a bread-making machine and fit the blade. Put the all the ingredients except the parsley, chilli and milk in the pan, following the order specified in the machine's manual. Add the mashed parsnips with the liquid. Fit the pan into the machine and close the lid. Set to the dough programme, adding the parsley and chilli when the machine beeps.

Turn the dough out on to a lightly floured surface at the end of the programme and cut it into 10 equal pieces. Shape each piece of dough into a ball and drop into an oiled 150 ml (¼ pint) dariole mould. Place the moulds on a baking sheet and cover loosely with oiled clingfilm. Leave in a warm place for 25–30 minutes, or until the dough has just risen above the tops of the moulds.

Brush the dough with the milk and bake in a preheated oven, 220°C (425°F), Gas Mark 7, for 10–15 minutes until golden and the bases of the bread sound hollow when tapped. Transfer to a wire rack to cool.

For carrot & onion loaves, boil 150 g (5 oz) peeled and roughly chopped carrots until just tender. Drain and mash, reserving 275 ml (9 fl oz) of the cooking liquid. Fry 1 small onion, chopped, in 1 tablespoon oil over a medium heat for 10 minutes until soft. Make the bread as above, using 250 g (8 oz) strong white bread flour and 200 g (7 oz) strong wholemeal bread flour in place of the white flour and the carrots and their liquid instead of the parsnips.

artichoke & roasted pepper pizza

Makes **2**

Preparation time **20 minutes**, plus proving

Cooking time **15 minutes**

200 g (7 oz) **strong white bread flour**, plus extra for dusting

7 g (¼ oz) sachet **fast-action dried yeast**

pinch of **salt**

3 tablespoons **olive oil**

just under 150 ml (¼ pint) **warm water**

150 ml (¼ pint) **passata**

1 **garlic clove**, crushed

1 teaspoon **oregano leaves**

1 tablespoon **semolina**

1 roasted **red pepper** from a can or jar, cut into wide strips

290 g (9 ¾ oz) jar marinated **artichokes** in oil, drained

50 g (2 oz) **black olives**

125 g (4 oz) **vegan mozzarella-style cheese**, grated

2 handfuls of **rocket leaves**

salt and **pepper**

Sift the flour into a bowl. Add the yeast to one side of the bowl and the salt to the other. Add 2 tablespoons of the oil and the measurement water and mix to form a dough, adding a little more water if the dough feels dry.

Tip the dough on to a lightly floured surface and knead for about 5 minutes until smooth and stretchy. Put the dough in a clean bowl, cover with clingfilm and leave to rise in a warm place for about 20 minutes.

Meanwhile, mix the passata, garlic and oregano together in a bowl and season with salt and pepper.

Turn the dough out on to a lightly floured surface and cut in half. Knead each piece lightly into a ball and roll out thinly to a 25 cm (10 inch) round. Place each round on a large baking sheet sprinkled with the semolina.

Spread the passata mixture over the dough rounds and arrange the pepper strips, artichokes and olives over the top in a thin layer. Scatter over the vegan cheese, drizzle over the remaining 1 tablespoon oil and bake in a preheated oven, 220°C (425°F), Gas Mark 7, for 12–15 minutes until the bases are crisp and golden. Top with the rocket leaves just before serving.

For courgette, harissa & red onion pizza, make
2 pizza bases and place each on a baking sheet sprinkled with semolina as above. Mix 275 ml (9 fl oz) passata and 1 teaspoon harissa together, spread over the pizza bases and top with 1 trimmed and thinly sliced courgette and 1 thinly sliced red onion. Scatter over 50 g (2 oz) black olives and 125 g (4 oz) grated vegan mozzarella-style cheese, then bake as above. Scatter with coriander leaves before serving.

minted courgette & lemon loaf

Makes **1 large loaf**
Preparation and cooking time
3–4 hours, depending on
machine, plus standing

1 large **courgette**, about
225 g (7½ oz), trimmed
2 tablespoons **salt**, plus
½ teaspoon
175 ml (6 fl oz) **water**
75 ml (3 fl oz) **olive oil**
½ teaspoon freshly ground
black pepper
400 g (13 oz) **strong white
bread flour**
1 tablespoon **caster sugar**
1¼ teaspoons **fast-action
dried yeast**
finely grated rind of 1 **lemon**
2 tablespoons chopped **mint**
3 tablespoons **capers**, rinsed
and drained

Grate the courgette coarsely and mix in a colander with the 2 tablespoons salt. Leave to stand for 30 minutes. Rinse the courgette in plenty of cold water, pat dry between several layers of kitchen paper and set aside.

Lift the bread pan out of a bread-making machine and fit the blade. Put all the ingredients except the lemon rind, mint and capers in the pan, following the order specified in the machine's manual.

Fit the pan into the machine and close the lid. Set to a 750 g (1½ lb) loaf size on the basic white programme. Select your preferred crust setting. Add the courgette, lemon rind, mint and capers when the machine beeps.

Remove the pan from the machine at the end of the programme and shake the bread out on to a wire rack to cool.

For carrot & spelt loaf with sesame, prepare the bread dough as above, using 1 large carrot, peeled and coarsely grated, in place of the courgette and using a mixture of 275 g (9 oz) strong white bread flour and 125 g (4 oz) spelt flour instead of all strong white flour. Set the bread-making machine as above, then when the machine beeps, add 3 tablespoons black or white sesame seeds and 2 tablespoons chopped parsley and proceed as above.

186

chocolate & beetroot fudge cake

Serves **12**
Preparation time **20 minutes**,
 plus cooling and chilling
Cooking time **45–50 minutes**

250 g (8 oz) **plain flour**
75 g (3 oz) **cocoa powder**
1 teaspoon **bicarbonate of
 soda**
300 g (10½ oz) **light
 muscovado sugar**
250 g (8 oz) **ready-cooked
 fresh beetroot** (not pickled),
 chopped
300 ml (½ pint) **almond milk**
100 ml (3½ fl oz) **sunflower
 oil**, plus extra for oiling
2 teaspoons **vanilla extract**
1 tablespoon **cider vinegar**
pink **edible sprinkles** or fresh
 unsprayed **rose petals**,
 washed and patted dry, to
 decorate

Frosting
150 g (5 oz) **vegan spread**
225 g (8 oz) **icing sugar**
1 teaspoon **vanilla extract**
150 g (5 oz) **dairy-free plain
 dark chocolate**, melted (see
 page 232) and cooled

Sift the flour, cocoa powder and bicarbonate of soda together into a large bowl. Stir in the muscovado sugar.

Blend the beetroot in a blender or food processor until smooth. With the motor running, pour in the almond milk, oil, vanilla and vinegar.

Pour the beetroot mixture on to the dry ingredients and stir until mixed. Pour into an oiled and base-lined 20 cm (8 inch) springform cake tin and bake in a preheated oven, 180°C (350°F), Gas Mark 4, for 45–50 minutes until just firm to the touch. Leave to cool in the tin.

Meanwhile, beat the spread, icing sugar and vanilla together for the frosting in an electric mixer until soft, then gradually beat in the melted chocolate until well combined and smooth. Refrigerate for 1 hour. Release the cooled cake from the tin, spread with the chilled icing and decorate with sprinkles or rose petals.

For double chocolate & courgette tray bake, sift 250 g (8 oz) plain flour, 75 g (3 oz) cocoa powder and 1 teaspoon bicarbonate of soda together into a large bowl. Stir in 350 g (11½ oz) light muscovado sugar. Mix together 300 ml (½ pint) each almond milk and sunflower oil, 2 teaspoons vanilla extract and 1 tablespoon cider vinegar in a jug. Coarsely grate 200 g (7 oz) courgette, squeezing out any excess moisture. Stir into the dry ingredients with the almond milk mixture and 100 g (3½ oz) dairy-free plain dark chocolate drops. Pour into an oiled and lined 18 x 28 cm (7 x 11 inch) shallow baking tin and bake in a preheated oven, 180°C (350°F), Gas Mark 4, for 25–30 minutes until just firm to the touch. Cut into squares and dust with icing sugar.

lemon & poppy seed cupcakes

Makes **12**
Preparation time **40 minutes**,
  plus cooling
Cooking time **20 minutes**

225 g (7½ oz) **plain flour**
2 teaspoons **baking powder**
¼ teaspoon **bicarbonate of
  soda**
½ teaspoon **salt**
125 g (4 oz) **caster sugar**
finely grated rind of 2 **lemons**
  and 1 tablespoon **lemon
  juice**
1 tablespoon **poppy seeds**,
  plus 1 teaspoon for
  decorating
75 ml (3 fl oz) **sunflower oil**
7 tablespoons **rice milk**

Frosting
125 g (4 oz) **vegan spread**
250 g (9 oz) **icing sugar**
finely grated rind of 1 **lemon**
a few drops of **yellow food
  colouring**

Sift the flour, baking powder, bicarbonate of soda and salt together into a large bowl. Stir in the sugar, lemon rind and poppy seeds.

Mix the oil, rice milk and lemon juice together in a jug. Add to the dry ingredients and stir to mix. Spoon evenly into a 12-hole muffin tin lined with paper cases and bake in a preheated oven, 160°C (325°F), Gas Mark 3, for 15 minutes until just firm to the touch. Leave to cool on a wire rack.

Beat the spread, icing sugar, lemon rind and food colouring for the frosting together in an electric mixer or in a bowl until soft and smooth. Spoon or pipe the frosting on to the cooled cakes and sprinkle with the remaining poppy seeds.

For rosewater & pistachio cupcakes, sift 225 g (7½ oz) plain flour, 2 teaspoons baking powder, ¼ teaspoon bicarbonate of soda and ½ teaspoon salt together into a large bowl. Stir in 125 g (4 oz) caster sugar and 50 g (2 oz) finely chopped pistachio nuts. Mix together 75 ml (3 fl oz) sunflower oil, 4 tablespoons rice milk, 1 tablespoon cider vinegar and 1 teaspoon rosewater in a jug. Add to the dry ingredients and stir to mix. Spoon evenly into a 12-hole muffin tin lined with paper cases and bake as above. Leave to cool on a wire rack. Beat 125 g (4 oz) vegan spread, 225 g (7½ oz) icing sugar and ½ teaspoon rosewater together in an electric mixer or in a bowl until soft and smooth. Spread or pipe over the cooled cupcakes and sprinkle with chopped pistachios to decorate.

sticky cinnamon & pecan buns

Makes **10**

Preparation time **45 minutes**, plus standing, proving and setting

Cooking time **30 minutes**

1 tablespoon ground **flaxseed**

200 ml (7 fl oz) **almond milk**

15 g (½ oz) **fast-action dried yeast**

450 g (14½ oz) **strong white bread flour**, plus extra for dusting

½ teaspoon **salt**

75 g (3 oz) **vegan spread**, cubed

50 g (2 oz) **soft light brown sugar**

125 g (4 oz) **icing sugar**

sunflower oil, for oiling

Filling

100 g (4 oz) **vegan spread**

8 tablespoons **soft light brown sugar**

2 teaspoons **ground cinnamon**

75 g (3 oz) **pecan nuts**, roughly chopped

6 fresh **Medjool dates**, stoned and mashed

2 tablespoons **maple syrup**

Mix the flaxseed with 3 tablespoons water in a small jug and set aside. Heat the almond milk gently in a saucepan until lukewarm. Stir in the yeast and leave to stand for 10 minutes.

Combine the flour and salt in a large bowl, add the spread and rub in with the fingertips until the mixture resembles fine breadcrumbs, then stir in the brown sugar. Mix the flaxseed mixture into the yeast mixture, then stir into the flour mixture and mix to a smooth, soft dough.

Tip the dough out on to a lightly floured surface and knead for about 5 minutes until smooth and elastic. Put in a clean bowl, cover with clingfilm and leave to rise in a warm place for 10 minutes.

Mix together the spread, sugar and cinnamon for the filling in a bowl until well combined. Add the pecan nuts, mashed dates and maple syrup and mix well.

Turn the dough out on to a lightly floured surface and knead for 2 minutes until smooth. Roll out to a rectangle about 30 x 45 cm (12 x 18 inches). Spread the filling evenly over the surface, then roll up tightly from one of the longer sides of the dough to form a spiral. Slice into 10 even slices, then place well spaced apart on a baking sheet, cover loosely with lightly oiled clingfilm and leave to prove in a warm place for 30 minutes.

Remove the clingfilm and bake in a preheated oven, 200°C (400°F), Gas Mark 6, for 25 minutes until golden and cooked through. Leave to cool on a wire rack. Put the icing sugar in a bowl, add 2 tablespoons water and mix until soft and smooth. Drizzle over the cooled buns and leave to set for 20 minutes before serving.

vanilla & jam shortbread

Makes **8**

Preparation time **30 minutes**, plus chilling

Cooking time **10–12 minutes**

125 g (4 oz) **vegan spread**
50 g (2 oz) **caster sugar**
150 g (5 oz) **plain flour**, plus extra for dusting
25 g (1 oz) **cornflour**
1 teaspoon **vanilla extract**
3 tablespoons **raspberry** or **strawberry jam**
icing sugar, for dusting

Beat the spread and caster sugar together in an electric mixer until pale and fluffy. Sift the flour and cornflour together into the mixture, add the vanilla and mix until combined. Roll the dough into a ball, wrap in clingfilm and chill for 30 minutes.

Roll the dough out on a lightly floured surface to about 5 mm (¼ inch) thick. Use a 5 cm (2 inch) square or round cutter to cut out 16 squares or rounds, rerolling the trimmings as necessary. Place on 2 baking sheets lined with baking parchment and bake in a preheated oven, 160°C (325°F), Gas Mark 3, for 10–12 minutes until pale golden.

Leave the shortbreads to cool on the sheets for 10 minutes until firm, then transfer to a wire rack to cool completely.

Sandwich the biscuits together with the jam and dust with icing sugar.

For jam & coconut streusel tarts, make the shortbread dough and chill as above. Roll the dough out as above, then use a 7 cm (3 inch) round cutter to cut out 12 rounds, rerolling the trimmings as necessary. Use the rounds to line 12 holes of a bun tin. Add a teaspoonful of raspberry or strawberry jam to each lined hole. Put 25 g (1 oz) plain flour, 75 g (3 oz) caster sugar, 50 g (2 oz) vegan spread and 3 tablespoons desiccated coconut in a bowl and rub together with the fingertips until crumbly. Sprinkle over the jam and bake in a preheated oven, 160°C (325°F), Gas Mark 3, for 15 minutes until golden.

cranberry scones & compote

Serves **6**

Preparation time **20 minutes**, plus standing and cooling

Cooking time **25 minutes**

6 tablespoons **soya milk**

1 tablespoon **cider vinegar**

1 tablespoon ground **golden flaxseed (linseed)**

275 g (9 oz) **plain flour,** plus extra for dusting

50 g (2 oz) **golden caster sugar**

1 teaspoon **baking powder**

½ teaspoon **bicarbonate of soda**

1 teaspoon ground **cinnamon**

125 g (4 oz) **vegan spread,** cubed, plus extra for greasing

125 g (4 oz) **dried cranberries**

1 tablespoon **demerara sugar**

Compote

125 g (4 oz) **strawberries,** hulled and quartered

2 tablespoons **caster sugar**

125 g (4 oz) **blackberries**

Mix 5 tablespoons of the soya milk, vinegar and flaxseed together in a jug, then leave to stand for 10 minutes (the mixture will separate slightly and turn thick).

Meanwhile, heat the strawberries and sugar for the compote in a saucepan over a gentle heat for 2–3 minutes until the sugar is dissolved. Add the blackberries and cook for a further 2–3 minutes until the fruit has softened and a juice has formed. Remove from the heat and leave to cool.

Put the flour in a large bowl and stir in the caster sugar, baking powder, bicarbonate of soda and cinnamon. Add the spread and rub in with the fingertips until the mixture resembles fine breadcrumbs. Stir in the cranberries, then add the soya milk mixture and mix to form a soft dough.

Roll the dough out on a lightly floured work surface to an 18 cm (7 inch) round and score into 6 wedges with a knife. Place on a lightly greased baking sheet, brush with the remaining soya milk and sprinkle with the demerara sugar. Bake in a preheated oven, 200°C (400°F), Gas Mark 6, for 15–18 minutes until golden and cooked through. Leave to cool slightly, then serve warm with the cooled compote.

For lemon & blueberry scones, finely grate the rind of 1 lemon, then squeeze the juice. Mix 5 tablespoons soya milk, 1 tablespoon ground golden flaxseed and the lemon juice together in a jug, then leave to stand for 10 minutes. Make the dough as above, stirring in the lemon rind and 125 g (4 oz) blueberries in place of the cranberries. Roll out on a lightly floured surface to a 20 cm (8 inch) round and score into 6 wedges. Place on a lightly greased baking sheet and bake as above. Serve warm.

stem ginger & dark choc cookies

Makes **14**
Preparation time **20 minutes**
Cooking time **15 minutes**

6 tablespoons **golden syrup**
50 g (2 oz) **vegan spread**
115 g (4 oz) **rolled oats**
75 g (3 oz) **wholemeal plain flour**
1 teaspoon **baking powder**
50 g (2 oz) well-drained **stem ginger** in syrup, finely chopped
50 g (2 oz) **plain dark chocolate** (70% cocoa solids), roughly chopped

Heat the golden syrup and spread in a small saucepan over a gentle heat until melted, stirring. Allow to cool slightly.

Mix all the remaining ingredients together in a large bowl. Pour in the syrup mixture and mix to form a soft dough. Place 14 spoonfuls of the mixture well spaced apart on a large baking sheet lined with baking parchment and gently press with the back of a spoon to flatten slightly. Bake in a preheated oven, 180°C (350°F), Gas Mark 4, for 8–10 minutes until pale golden.

Leave the cookies to cool on the baking sheet for 5 minutes until firm, then transfer to a wire rack to cool completely.

For spiced hazelnut & raisin cookies, melt the golden syrup and vegan spread as above. Mix together 75 g (3 oz) each rolled oats, wholemeal plain flour and raisins, 50 g (2 oz) lightly toasted and chopped hazelnuts and 1 teaspoon each baking powder and ground mixed spice in a large bowl. Pour in the syrup mixture and mix to form a soft dough. Continue with the recipe above to form, bake and cool the cookies.

sugarless fruit granola bars

Makes **9**

Preparation time **20 minutes**,
plus cooling

Cooking time **40 minutes**

225 g (7 ½ oz) peeled, cored
and roughly chopped
dessert apple

1 tablespoon **lemon juice**

1 tablespoon **agave syrup**

½ teaspoon ground **cinnamon**

sunflower oil, for oiling

Granola

125 g (4 oz) **rolled oats**

125 g (4 oz) **ready-to-eat
dried apricots**

125 g (4 oz) fresh **Medjool
dates**, stoned and roughly
chopped

2 tablespoons **ground
flaxseed (linseed)**

2 tablespoons **smooth peanut
butter**

55 ml (2 fl oz) **agave syrup**

Line a baking sheet with baking parchment. Toss the apple with the lemon juice, agave syrup and cinnamon in a bowl, then spread out on the lined baking sheet and roast in a preheated oven, 160°C (325°F), Gas Mark 3, for 20 minutes. Remove from the oven and leave to cool.

Increase the oven temperature to 180°C (350°F), Gas Mark 4. Pulse all the ingredients for the granola together in a food processor a few times until mixed and mashed. Fold in the cooled roasted apple, then spoon into a lightly oiled 20 cm (8 inch) square shallow cake tin and level with the back of a spoon. Bake in the oven for 20 minutes.

Leave to cool for 15 minutes before cutting into 9 squares to serve.

For pear, banana & hazelnut granola bars, toss 225 g (7 ½ oz) peeled, cored and chopped pear with 1 tablespoon each lemon juice and agave syrup in a bowl, then spread out on a baking sheet lined with baking parchment and roast in a preheated oven, 180°C (350°F), Gas Mark 4 for 20 minutes. Remove from the oven and leave to cool, keeping the oven on. Pulse together 125 g (4 oz) each rolled oats and fresh Medjool dates, stoned and roughly chopped, 1 small ripe banana, roughly chopped, 2 tablespoons each ground flaxseed (linseed) and toasted blanched hazelnuts and 55 ml (2 fl oz) agave syrup in a food processor a few times until mixed and mashed. Fold in the cooled roasted pear, then bake, cool and cut into squares as above.

desserts

banana & strawberry ice cream

Serves **6**

Preparation time **30 minutes**, plus freezing

525 g (17¼ oz) carton **vanilla soya custard**

250 ml (8 fl oz) **pot soya cream**

3 **bananas**, roughly chopped

175 g (6 oz) hulled **strawberries**

3 tablespoons **maple syrup**

Blend the custard, cream, bananas, half the strawberries and the maple syrup together in a blender or food processor until smooth.

Pour the mixture into a freezer-proof container and freeze for 3 hours until just starting to freeze around the edges.

Scrape the mixture into a bowl and beat with a stick blender until smooth. Finely chop the remaining strawberries, stir into the mixture and pour back into the freezer-proof container. Freeze for 3–4 hours or overnight until firm. Allow to soften for 15 minutes before serving.

For choc chip banana ice cream, blend the vanilla soya custard, soya cream and bananas as above with 2 tablespoons cocoa powder. Partially freeze and then whisk until smooth as above. Stir in 75 g (3 oz) plain dark chocolate chips before freezing until firm as above.

lemon & mint granita

Serves **6**
Preparation time **20 minutes**,
   plus cooling and freezing
Cooking time **5 minutes**

200 g (7 oz) **caster sugar**
300 ml (½ pint) **water**, plus
   extra to top up
pared rind and juice of
   3 **lemons**
25 g (1 oz) **mint sprigs**, plus
   a few tiny sprigs for
   decorating
icing sugar, for dusting

Heat the sugar, measurement water and lemon rind in a saucepan over a gentle heat until the sugar is dissolved. Increase the heat and boil for 2 minutes, then remove the pan from the heat.

Tear the tips off the mint stems and finely chop to give about 3 tablespoons, then reserve. Add the larger mint leaves and stems to the hot syrup and leave for 1 hour to cool and for the flavours to develop.

Strain the syrup through a sieve into a jug, add the chopped mint and top up to 600 ml (1 pint) with the lemon juice and extra cold water. Pour into a small roasting tin and freeze the mixture for 2–3 hours, or until mushy.

Break up the ice crystals with a fork, then return to the freezer for a further 2–3 hours, breaking up with a fork once or twice more until the mixture is the consistency of crushed ice.

Spoon into glass tumblers and decorate with tiny mint sprigs dusted with icing sugar before serving, or leave in the freezer until required. If leaving in the freezer, allow to soften for 15 minutes before serving. If frozen overnight or longer, break up with a fork before serving.

For iced ruby grapefruit granita, make a plain sugar syrup as above, omitting the lemon rind, then leave to cool, omitting the mint. Halve 4 ruby grapefruits, squeeze the juice and then reserve 4 of the grapefruit shell halves, scooping out and discarding any remaining flesh and membranes. Add the grapefruit juice to the syrup instead of the lemon juice, then freeze as above. Serve the granita spooned into the grapefruit shells.

lavender & rosemary sorbet

Serves **8**
Preparation time **25 minutes**,
  plus cooling and freezing
Cooking time **30 minutes**

225 g (7½ oz) **golden
  granulated sugar**
850 ml (1½ pints) **water**
6 tablespoons **elderflower
  cordial**
4 tablespoons **lavender
  flowers**
2 tablespoons **rosemary
  leaves**

Put the sugar in a saucepan with the measurement water, elderflower cordial, lavender and rosemary and bring to the boil. Boil for 8–10 minutes until the liquid has reduced by a third and become syrupy but without taking on any colour. Remove from the heat and leave to cool completely.

Strain the cooled syrup through a sieve into a freezer-proof container and freeze for about 4–5 hours until firm. Remove from the freezer and cut into chunks, then use a stick blender to beat until smooth. Return to the freezer and freeze again for about 3–4 hours or overnight until firm. The sorbet is now ready to serve, but allow to soften for 15 minutes before serving.

For strawberry sorbet, make the syrup as above and leave to cool. Blend 450 g (14½ oz) hulled strawberries in a blender or food processor until smooth. Pour the syrup into the strawberries and mix well, then transfer to a freezer-proof container. Freeze, then beat until smooth and refreeze as above.

summer berry sorbet

Serves **2**

Preparation time **5 minutes**, plus freezing

250 g (8 oz) **frozen mixed summer berries**
75 ml (3 fl oz) **spiced berry cordial**
2 tablespoons **Kirsch**
1 tablespoon **lime juice**

Put a shallow plastic container in the freezer to chill. Process the frozen berries, cordial, Kirsch and lime juice in a food processor or blender to a smooth purée. Be careful not to over-process, as this will soften the mixture too much.

Spoon into the chilled container and freeze for at least 25 minutes. Spoon into serving bowls and serve

For raspberry sorbet, replace the main recipe ingredients with frozen raspberries, elderflower cordial, crème de cassis and lemon juice. Use the same quantities and method as the summer berry sorbet.

melon, ginger & lime sorbet

Serves **4**

Preparation time **15 minutes**,
    plus cooling and freezing

1 large ripe **Charentais** or
    Galia melon, chilled
150 g (5 oz) **caster sugar**
1 teaspoon peeled and finely
    grated **fresh root ginger**
juice of 2 **limes**

Cut the melon in half and remove and discard the seeds, then roughly chop the flesh – you need about 450 g (14½ oz). Place in a food processor with the sugar, ginger and lime juice, then blend until smooth.

Transfer the sorbet to an ice cream maker and process according to the manufacturer's instructions. If you don't have an ice cream maker, place the mixture in a freezer-proof container and freeze for about 2–3 hours or until ice crystals have appeared on the surface. Beat with a hand-held electric whisk until smooth, then return to the freezer. Repeat this process twice more until you have a fine-textured sorbet and freeze until firm.

Remove the sorbet from the freezer 10 minutes before serving. Serve, scooped into glasses with a wafer.

For honeydew melon granita, place 75 g (3 oz) caster sugar in a saucepan with 150 ml (¼ pint) water and stir over a low heat until dissolved, then bring to the boil. Remove from the heat and leave to cool, then place in a food processor with 450 g (14½ oz) chopped Honeydew melon flesh and 2 tablespoons melon liqueur (optional) and blend until smooth. Transfer to a shallow freezer-proof container and freeze for 1 hour or until ice crystals appear at the edges. Stir the ice into the centre and return to the freezer. Stir and refreeze a few more times until frozen all over. To serve, scrape the granita with a fork and serve immediately.

spiced baked figs

Serves **4**
Preparation time **10 minutes**
Cooking time **15–20 minutes**

6 ripe **figs**, halved
1 **cinnamon stick**, broken
   in half
2 tablespoons **agave nectar**
2 tablespoons **brandy**
150 g (5 oz) **raspberries**
finely grated rind of **1 orange**
150 g (5 oz) **natural soya
   yogurt**

Arrange the fig halves, cut-side up, in a baking dish with the cinnamon. Drizzle over 1 tablespoon of the agave nectar and the brandy.

Bake in a preheated oven, 190°C (375°F), Gas Mark 5, for 15–20 minutes until soft. Sprinkle over the raspberries and turn to coat in the juices, then leave to cool slightly.

Mix the remaining agave nectar with the orange rind and soya yogurt and serve with the figs and raspberries.

For spiced fig & orange tarte tatin, heat 2 tablespoons agave nectar in a round flameproof, ovenproof dish on the hob. Add ½ teaspoon ground cinnamon and the finely grated rind of 1 orange and stir to mix, then place 6 halved ripe figs, cut-side down, in the dish. Cover with a sheet of ready-rolled vegan puff pastry, tucking in the edges. Bake in a preheated oven, 200°C (400°F), Gas Mark 6, for 25–30 minutes until well risen and golden. Carefully invert the dish on to a plate with a rim to catch the juices. Serve warm with natural soya yogurt or vegan ice cream.

vanilla-spiced fruit salad

Serves **4**

Preparation time **10 minutes**, plus cooling

Cooking time **8 minutes**

150 ml (¼ pint) **apple juice**

1 **vanilla pod**, slit in half lengthways

2 tablespoons **agave nectar** or **soft light brown sugar**

2 **kiwi fruit**, peeled and sliced

250 g (8 oz) **strawberries**, hulled and thickly sliced

125 g (4 oz) **blueberries**

1 ripe **mango**, peeled, stoned and sliced

mint leaves, to decorate

Warm the apple juice in a small saucepan with the split vanilla pod and agave nectar or sugar over a gentle heat. Simmer gently for 4–5 minutes, then leave to cool completely. Remove the vanilla pod and scrape the seeds into the light syrup.

Combine the fruits in a large bowl and drizzle over the vanilla-spiced syrup. Stir gently to coat, then spoon into serving bowls and sprinkle with mint leaves to decorate.

For Asian-style fruit salad, simmer 150 ml (¼ pint) pineapple juice in a saucepan with 2 star anise, 1 tablespoon lime juice, 2 cloves and the agave nectar as above. Leave to cool, then chill for 1 hour. Cut off the top and base of 1 small pineapple and slice off the skin. Cut the pineapple into quarters and remove the core from each quarter. Cut into slices and combine with 1 peeled, stoned and sliced mango, a drained 400 g (13 oz) can lychees and 2 sliced star fruits in a serving bowl. Pour over the syrup and serve.

coconut rice pudding

Serves **4**

Preparation time **15 minutes**

Cooking time **1½ hours**

75 g (3 oz) **Thai fragrant** or
pudding rice

50 g (2 oz) **caster sugar**

400 ml (14 fl oz) can **coconut
milk**

1 ripe **mango**, peeled, stoned
and chopped

finely grated rind and juice of
1 lime

Put the rice in a saucepan with the sugar and coconut milk. Refill the coconut milk can with water and add to the pan.

Bring the mixture to the boil, stirring, then pour into a shallow 1.5 litre (2½ pint) ovenproof dish. Bake in a preheated oven, 150°C (300°F), Gas Mark 2, for 1 hour 25 minutes, stirring occasionally, until the rice is tender and the liquid is absorbed.

Mix the mango and lime rind and juice together in a bowl and serve with the warm or cold rice pudding.

For coconut rice pudding brûlee, bring the rice, sugar, coconut milk and water to the boil, stirring, as above, then leave to simmer on the hob, stirring occasionally, for 20 minutes until the rice is tender and the liquid is absorbed. Spoon the mixture into individual heatproof dishes, level the surface and leave to cool. Chill for 2–3 hours or overnight. Just before serving, sprinkle 1 tablespoon demerara sugar evenly over the surface of each dish. Place under a hot grill or use a cook's blowtorch to melt and caramelize the sugar. Leave to cool for 10 minutes to harden the caramel before serving with chopped mango or rhubarb compote.

blueberry & pear slump

Serves **4**
Preparation time **20 minutes**
Cooking time **25–30 minutes**

2 large ripe **pears**, peeled,
  cored and chopped
200 g (7 oz) **blueberries**
5 tablespoons **caster sugar**
175 g (6 oz) **plain flour**
1 teaspoon **baking powder**
50 g (2 oz) **ground almonds**
25 g (1 oz) **vegan spread**,
  diced
150 ml (5 fl oz) **almond milk**
25 g (1 oz) **flaked almonds**

Divide the pears and blueberries between 4 large ramekins and sprinkle with 2 tablespoons of the sugar.

Sift the flour and baking powder together into a bowl and stir in the ground almonds and 2 tablespoons of the remaining sugar. Add the spread and rub in with the fingertips. Stir in the almond milk to make a sticky dough.

Dot small spoonfuls of the dough over the fruit and sprinkle over the remaining 1 tablespoon sugar and the flaked almonds. Bake in a preheated oven, 190°C (375°F), Gas Mark 5, for 25–30 minutes until the fruit is soft and the topping is golden.

For rhubarb, plum & orange slump, chop 250 g (8 oz) each rhubarb and plums and divide between 4 large ramekins. Sprinkle with 2 tablespoons caster sugar. Sift 175 g (6 oz) plain flour and 2 teaspoons baking powder together into a bowl and stir in 50 g (2 oz) ground almonds, 2 tablespoons caster sugar and the finely grated rind of 1 orange. Rub in 25 g (1 oz) diced vegan spread with the fingertips, then stir in 200 ml (7 fl oz) almond milk to make a soft dough. Dot spoonfuls of the mixture over the fruit and sprinkle with 1 tablespoon caster sugar and 25 g (1 oz) flaked almonds. Bake as above.

poached peaches & raspberries

Serves **6**

Preparation time **15 minutes**

Cooking time **25 minutes**

250 ml (8 fl oz) **water**

150 ml (¼ pint) **Marsala** or **sweet sherry**

75 g (3 oz) **caster sugar**

1 **vanilla pod**

6 ripe **peaches**, halved and stoned

150 g (5 oz) **raspberries**

Pour the measurement water and Marsala or sherry into a saucepan and add the sugar. Slit the vanilla pod in half lengthways and scrape out the seeds into the pan, then add the pod. Heat gently until the sugar is dissolved.

Arrange the peach halves, cut-side up, in an ovenproof dish so that they sit together snugly. Pour over the hot syrup, then cover and cook in a preheated oven, 180°F (350°F), Gas Mark 4, for 20 minutes.

Scatter over the raspberries and serve the fruit either warm or cold. Spoon into serving bowls and decorate with the vanilla pod cut into thin strips.

For poached prunes with vanilla, make the sugar syrup as above, then add 250 g (8 oz) pitted prunes instead of the peaches. Cover and simmer as above, then serve with spoonfuls of natural soya yogurt or cream and 4 crumbled vegan cookies.

apple with salted caramel sauce

Serves **4**
Preparation **5 minutes**
Cooking time **15 minutes**

50 g (2 oz) **vegan spread**
4 **dessert apples**, quartered,
  cored and sliced
50 g (2 oz) **light muscovado
  sugar**
50 g (2 oz) stoned fresh
  Medjool dates, chopped
100 ml (3½ fl oz) **vegan
  cream**
2 tablespoons **cold water**
½ teaspoon **sea salt flakes**

Melt the spread in a frying pan, add the apples and cook over a medium heat for 2 minutes until starting to soften.

Add the sugar and stir until melted. Add the dates, toss and cook for a few seconds. Pour in the vegan cream and cook, stirring constantly, for 2 minutes to make a caramel sauce.

Stir in the measurement cold water and heat over a low heat until the sauce is smooth, then add the salt flakes and mix well. Serve warm with vegan cream or ice cream.

For toffee apple flapjack crumble, soften the apples, omitting the dates, and make the caramel sauce as above, then spoon into an ovenproof dish. Melt 75 g (3 oz) vegan spread with 75 g (3 oz) demerara sugar and 1 tablespoon golden syrup in a saucepan. Add 125 g (4 oz) porridge oats and 50 g (2 oz) self-raising flour and stir well, then spoon over the apples and caramel. Bake in a preheated oven, 180°C (350°F), Gas Mark 4, for 25–30 minutes until golden.

banana fritters & cinnamon sugar

Serves **4**
Preparation time **20 minutes**, plus standing
Cooking time **5 minutes**

225 g (7½oz) **plain flour**
½ teaspoon **ground nutmeg**
2 teaspoons **ground cinnamon**
375 ml (13 fl oz) **sparkling water**
sunflower oil, for deep-frying
4 **bananas**, halved both lengthways and widthways
3 tablespoons **demerara sugar**
1 tablespoon **caster sugar**

Mix the flour, nutmeg and 1 teaspoon of the cinnamon together in a bowl, then make a well in the centre. Gradually add and whisk in enough of the sparkling water to make a smooth batter thick enough to coat the back of a spoon. Leave to stand for 20 minutes.

Fill a deep-sided saucepan one-third full with oil and heat to 180–190°C (350–375°F), or until a cube of bread browns in 30 seconds. Using a pair of tongs, dip the banana pieces, in batches, into the batter, gently lower into the hot oil and cook for 30 seconds–1 minute until golden and crisp, taking care not to overcrowd the pan with too many at a time, as they will stick together and the oil temperature will drop. Remove from the pan with a slotted spoon and drain on kitchen paper.

Mix the sugars with the cinnamon, then scatter over the hot fritters to serve.

For apple & pear fritters with spiced sugar, make the batter and leave to stand as above. Peel, core and quarter 3 dessert apples and 2 pears. Heat the oil as above. Using a pair of tongs, dip the apple and pear pieces, in batches, into the batter, gently lower into the hot oil and cook for 2 minutes until golden. Remove from the pan with a slotted spoon and drain on kitchen paper. Mix 5 tablespoons caster sugar with 1 teaspoon ground cinnamon and ½ teaspoon ground mixed spice, then scatter over the hot fritters to serve.

papaya with tumbling berries

Serves **4**
Preparation time **10 minutes**

2 large ripe **papayas**
125 g (4 oz) **blueberries**
125 g (4 oz) **raspberries**
250 g (8 oz) hulled
   strawberries, sliced
125 g (4 oz) **cherries**, pitted
   (optional)
agave syrup, to taste
   (optional)
lime wedges, to serve

Cut the papayas in half and scoop out the seeds and discard. Place each half on a serving plate.

Mix the blueberries, raspberries, strawberries and cherries, if using, together in a bowl and then pile into the papaya halves.

Drizzle with a little agave syrup, if liked, and serve with lime wedges.

For papaya & berry smoothie, peel and halve 2 large ripe papayas, then remove and discard the seeds and cut the flesh into chunks. Put in a blender or food processor with the remaining fruits as above and 10 ice cubes. Add 500 ml (17 fl oz) apple or guava juice and blend until smooth. Pour into glasses and serve immediately.

champagne & raspberry jellies

Serves **4**
Preparation time **15 minutes**,
plus standing, cooling and
chilling
Cooking time **5 minutes**

200 ml (7 fl oz) **Champagne**
6 g (¼ oz) sachet **vegetarian
gelling powder**
150 ml (¼ pint) **apple and
raspberry juice**
1 tablespoon **caster sugar**
75 g (3 oz) **raspberries**
mint sprigs, to decorate
(optional)

Pour the Champagne into a jug, sprinkle over the gelling powder and set aside to dissolve.

Heat the apple and raspberry juice and sugar in a small saucepan and bring to the boil. Remove from the heat, then pour over the gelling powder mixture and mix well. Leave to cool for 20 minutes.

Divide the raspberries between 4 glasses and pour over the Champagne and juice mixture. Refrigerate for 3–4 hours or overnight until set. Serve with a thin layer of soya cream on the top if liked, although these jellies are really refreshing served with just a sprig of mint.

For spiced cranberry jellies, place 300 ml (½ pint) cranberry juice in a small saucepan with a broken cinnamon stick and bring to the boil. Remove from the heat and leave to cool and allow the flavours to infuse. Meanwhile, scatter a 6 g (¼ oz) sachet of vegetarian gelling powder over 50 ml (2 fl oz) of additional cranberry juice and set aside for 5 minutes to dissolve. Once the spiced cranberry juice is cool enough to touch, remove the cinnamon, pour over the gelling powder mixture and mix well. Divide 75 g (3 oz) cranberries between 4 glasses, pour over the cranberry juice mixture and refrigerate for 3–4 hours or overnight until set.

ultra-rich chocolate stacks

Serves **4**

Preparation time **20 minutes**, plus chilling

150 g (5 oz) **plain dark chocolate** (90% cocoa solids), broken into pieces

125 ml (4 fl oz) **coconut cream**

1 tablespoon **mint leaves**

125 g (4 oz) **raspberries**

½ teaspoon **cocoa powder**

½ teaspoon **icing sugar**

Put the chocolate pieces in a heatproof bowl and set over a saucepan of hot water. Stir until melted.

Spoon 12 spoonfuls of the melted chocolate on to a baking sheet lined with baking parchment and allow to spread into about 7 cm (3 inch) discs, then refrigerate for 30 minutes until set.

Whip the coconut cream in a bowl until thick. Layer 3 chocolate discs on each of 4 serving plates with the coconut cream, mint leaves and raspberries.

Mix the cocoa and icing sugar together, then dredge over the chocolate stacks to serve.

For chocolate & orange stacks, melt the chocolate as above, then stir in the finely grated rind of 1 orange. Spoon on to a lined baking sheet and refrigerate until set as above. Whip the coconut cream as above, then use to layer the discs in stacks of 3 along with a well-drained 300 g (10 oz) can mandarin segments in juice. Dredge with cocoa powder to serve.

stuffed spiced roasted pears

Serves **4**

Preparation time **20 minutes**

Cooking time **35 minutes**

4 ripe **pears**, preferably a pale-
skinned variety

3 ready-to-eat **pitted prunes**,
roughly chopped

25 g (1 oz) roasted **hazelnuts,**
roughly chopped

75 g (3 oz) **blackberries,**
halved

½ teaspoon **ground
cinnamon**

4 tablespoons **maple syrup**

25 g (1 oz) **vegan spread**

Halve the pears and then remove a small slice from
the back of each so that they sit level in a roasting tin.
Scoop out the core and seeds, leaving the stalk intact.

Mix the prunes and hazelnuts with the cinnamon and
maple syrup in a bowl, then fold in the blackberries. Pile
into the pear cavities and top each with a small knob of
the vegan spread. Cover the roasting tin with foil and
bake in a preheated oven, 200°C (400°F), Gas Mark 6,
for 25 minutes.

Remove the foil and roast for a further 10 minutes.
Serve with the juices spooned over the pears along with
a scoop of soya ice cream or yogurt, if liked.

For stuffed roasted apples with agave syrup, peel
4 apples, cut each in half and scoop out the core,
leaving the stalk intact. Remove a small slice from the
back of each apple half so that it sits level in a roasting
tin. Mix 2 roughly chopped dried figs and 25 g (1 oz)
lightly roasted Marcona almonds with 4 tablespoons
agave syrup in a bowl, then fold in 50 g (2 oz)
raspberries. Spoon into the apple cavities and cover
the tin with foil. Bake and then serve as above.

index

acknowledgements

Executive editor: Eleanor Maxfield
Text editor: Jo Richardson
Art direction and design: Penny Stock
Photographer: William Shaw
Home economist: Emma Frost
Stylist: Kim Sullivan
Production controller: Sarah Kramer

Photography copyright © Octopus Publishing Group Limited/William Shaw, except the following: copyright © Octopus Publishing Group/Stephen Conroy 73; Will Heap 91, 103, 209, 221; William Lingwood 97; William Reavell 63, 69; Ian Wallace 133, 139, 147, 171, 173.